Human Data Understanding
Sensors, Models, Knowledge

Vol. 2

T0135461

Human Data Understanding
Sensors, Models, Knowledge

Volume 2

Herausgegeben von

Prof. Dr.-Ing. Frank Deinzer
Hochschule für angewandte Wissenschaften
Würzburg-Schweinfurt

Prof. Dr.-Ing. Marcin Grzegorzek
Universität zu Lübeck

Frédéric Li

Deep Learning for Time-series Classification Enhanced by Transfer Learning Based on Sensor Modality Discrimination

Logos Verlag Berlin

λογος

Bibliographic information published by Die Deutsche Bibliothek

Die Deutsche Bibliothek lists this publication in the Deutsche National-
bibliografie; detailed bibliographic data is available in the Internet at
http://dnb.d-nb.de.

ISBN 978-3-8325-5396-8
ISSN 2701-9446

Logos Verlag Berlin GmbH
Georg-Knorr-Str. 4, Gebäude 10
12681 Berlin
Tel.:   +49 (0)30 / 42 85 10 90
Fax: +49 (0)30 / 42 85 10 92
http://www.logos-verlag.de

UNIVERSITÄT ZU LÜBECK

From the Institute of Medical Informatics
of the University of Lübeck
Director: Prof. Dr. rer. nat. habil. Heinz Handels

"Deep Learning for Time-series Classification Enhanced by Transfer Learning Based on Sensor Modality Discrimination"

Dissertation
for Fulfillment of
Requirements
for the Doctoral Degree
of the University of Lübeck

from the Department of Computer Sciences and Technical
Engineering

Submitted by

Frédéric Li
from Nancy, France

Lübeck 2021

First referee: Prof. Dr.-Ing. habil. Marcin Grzegorzek

Second referee: Prof. Dr. rer. nat. Esfandiar Mohammadi

Third referee: Prof. Dr.-Ing. habil. Alfred Mertins

Date of oral examination: 14.09.2021

Approved for printing: Lübeck, 20.09.2021

Acknowledgements

This PhD thesis is the conclusion of several years of research work carried out in both the (no longer existing) Research Group for Pattern Recognition of the University of Siegen (Germany) and the Medical Data Science of the University of Lübeck (Germany). This journey would not have been possible without the support of many people that I would like to thank here.

I would first like to thank my direct PhD supervisor Prof. Dr.-Ing. habil. Marcin Grzegorzek who accepted and integrated me in his research group(s) in both Siegen and Lübeck, provided me numerous opportunities to work on a wide variety of interesting projects connected to medical applications of ubiquitous computing, and supported me - both professionally and personally - whenever help was needed.

I would also like to thank my colleagues - PhD students, post-docs, student assistants - who accompanied me in this journey - in both Siegen and Lübeck. They contributed to creating a work environment fostering effective research and exchanges of ideas, which led over the last years to many collaborations on research projects related to various application domains of ubiquitous computing. Among those colleagues, I would especially like to show my gratitude to Prof. Dr.-Ing. Kimiaki Shirahama, who was always there to provide advice and critical feedback, and whose scientific guidance turned out to be invaluable.

Last but not least, I would like to thank my close relatives - and in particular my parents - who encouraged me in pursuing a PhD, and provided me with support and wise pieces of advice based on their own experience during those past years of work.

Abstract

Computers have become increasingly present in our daily lives over the past years, thanks to several converging factors such as the development of highly efficient hardware in terms of storage and computational power capabilities, or the trivialisation of keeping portable computing devices - such as smartphones - on oneself at all times. This trend - already predicted decades ago by the founder of *ubiquitous computing* Mark Weiser - has led to an increase in unobtrusive and invisible wearable sensors, facilitating the process of acquiring data, and especially time-series ones. At the same time, remarkable progress in the development of even more effective machine learning techniques has been observed over the past decades, notably regarding approaches to learn relevant *features* to provide an abstracted representation of the data. The most notable phenomenon illustrating this trend is the fast rise in popularity of *deep learning*, which refers to machine learning using Deep Neural Networks (DNNs), and is reputed to yield remarkable performances when large amounts of data are available. The conjunction of those two trends has opened up various new possibilities of application as evidenced by the growing research community of ubiquitous computing.

Despite this favourable context, the application of machine learning approaches - and more specifically deep learning - still faces obstacles. The success of obtaining a proper machine learning model strongly hinges on the quality and quantity of data used to train it. On the one hand, most breakthroughs using DNNs over the past years have been made in application fields using images thanks to the availability of very large benchmark image datasets such as *ImageNet*. On the other hand, time-series data - which represent the most common type of data in ubiquitous computing application - remain scarce: data acquisition campaigns with wearable sensors are costly in terms of time and resources in practice, and the large diversity in types of time-series data acquired by different sensors makes the building of an equivalent of ImageNet for time-series difficult. While deep learning using time-series data has already been successfully applied in various contexts in past studies, their scope is usually limited to their specific application field, and not always rigorously compared with other state-of-the-art machine learning approaches.

In this context, this thesis proposes to explore the topic of using deep learning for time-series classification, which is one of the most commonly encountered machine learning problems in ubiquitous computing applications. It attempts in particular to provide elements of answer to two questions which have not been fully addressed in the literature: 1. Is it beneficial to use deep learning for time-series classification over other traditional machine learning approaches when data are limited or scarce? 2. Is there a way to bypass data scarcity issues to enhance the performances of DNNs for time-series classification? The thesis is structured as follows: after an introduction presenting the context with more details and providing examples illustrating the difficulties of applying deep learning in practice, each question is investigated more closely in one dedicated Chapter.

The first part of the thesis (Chapter 2) explores the first of the two aforementioned questions in the context of sensor-based Human Activity Recognition (HAR). Sensor-based HAR has established itself as the most popular application of ubiquitous computing due to its numerous potential applications in real-life, the affordability and the pervasiveness of motion-based sensors, and the simplicity of data annotation which has led to relatively higher amounts of available data. The Chapter focuses more specifically on the question of how to obtain proper feature representations of the data for HAR. While abundant, the sensor-based HAR literature on this topic has so far been mostly scattered, with little efforts to compare the performances of the different approaches on a fair basis. In this Chapter, a comparative study between various state-of-the-art feature extraction approaches - supervised or unsupervised, centred around feature engineering or feature learning with DNNs - is detailed. An evaluation framework allowing a strict comparison is firstly defined and used to carry out extensive experiments on two sensor-based HAR benchmark datasets: *OPPORTUNITY* and *UniMiB-SHAR*. The results highlighted three main phenomena: the superiority of supervised feature learning approaches over unsupervised ones, the dominance of methods using deep learning to learn features over those relying on manual feature engineering in all tested configurations, and the effectiveness of hybrid DNN models combining convolutional and recurrent layers. The study therefore validates the effectiveness of deep learning for time-series classification in the context of sensor-based HAR.

The second part of this thesis (Chapter 3) focuses on time-series *transfer learning* to bypass data scarcity issues and enhance the performances of DNNs for time-series classification. Transfer learning has become state-of-the-art when image modalities are involved due to its proven and repeated ability to let DNNs yield better classification performances than without transfer. Time-series transfer learning however still remains relatively unexplored due to lower quantities of available time-series data, and large differences in data formats depending on which sensors were used to acquire them. Several transfer methods have been proposed in the literature, but their scope is usually limited either to specific application fields, to strict conditions of similarity between the *source* and *target domains*, or to single-channel time-series data. A new time-series transfer learning approach addressing those issues was developed in the frame of this thesis. It proposes to use sensor modality classification as an auxiliary task to learn general transferable time-series features. Time-series datasets related to various applications of ubiquitous computing are firstly aggregated to build a source domain. A DNN processing single-channel data (sDNN) is trained to recognise sensor modalities, and its weights are then transferred to a DNN architecture processing multichannel time-series (mDNN) on the target domain. The mDNN is finally fine-tuned on the target domain to solve the target problem. This process can be applied to any target domain using multichannel time-series data no matter how many channels were used, thus addressing the limitations of existing approaches. Experiments carried out for two distinct target applications of ubiquitous computing - sensor based HAR and Emotion Recognition - showed that the proposed transfer approach yields classification performance improvements compared to not using any transfer. Such results indicate its strong potential for applications of ubiquitous computing relying on time-series classification.

Zusammenfassung

Computer sind in den letzten Jahren in unserem täglichen Leben, dank mehrerer konvergierender Faktoren wie der Entwicklung hocheffizienter Hardware in Bezug auf Speicher- und Rechenleistung oder der Möglichkeit, tragbare Computergeräte - wie Smartphones - ständig bei sich zu haben, immer präsenter geworden. Dieser Trend - bereits vor Jahrzehnten von Mark Weiser, dem Begründer des Ubiquitous Computing, vorausgesagt - hat zu einer Zunahme von unauffälligen und unsichtbaren tragbaren Sensoren geführt, die die Erfassung von Daten, insbesondere von Zeitreihen, erleichtern. Gleichzeitig wurden in den letzten Jahrzehnten bemerkenswerte Fortschritte bei der Entwicklung noch effektiverer maschineller Lerntechniken beobachtet, insbesondere in Bezug auf Ansätze zum Erlernen relevanter Merkmale, um eine abstrahierte Darstellung der Daten zu erhalten. Besonders hervorgehoben wird dies durch den aktuellen Trend und schnellen Anstieg der Popularität von Deep Learning, das auf maschinelles Lernen unter Verwendung von Deep Neural Networks (DNNs) beruht und dem nachgesagt wird bemerkenswerte Leistungen zu erzielen, falls große Datenmengen verfügbar sind. Die Verbindung dieser beiden Trends hat verschiedene neue Anwendungsmöglichkeiten eröffnet, wie die wachsende Forschungsgemeinschaft des Ubiquitous Computing beweist.

Trotz dieser günstigen Ausgangssituation stößt die Anwendung von Ansätzen des maschinellen Lernens - und insbesondere des Deep Learnings - immer noch auf Hindernisse. Der Erfolg eines geeigneten Modells hängt stark von der Qualität und Quantität der zum Training verwendeten Daten ab. Einerseits wurden die meisten Durchbrüche mit DNNs in den letzten Jahren in Anwendungsbereichen erzielt, die Bilder verwenden, dank der Verfügbarkeit von sehr großen Benchmark-Bilddatensätzen wie *ImageNet*. Auf der anderen Seite sind Zeitreihendaten - die die häufigste Art von Daten in Ubiquitous-Computing-Anwendungen darstellen - nach wie vor rar: Datenerfassungskampagnen mit tragbaren Sensoren sind in der Praxis zeitaufwendig- und ressourcenintensiv, und die große Vielfalt an Arten von Zeitreihendaten, die von verschiedenen Sensoren erfasst werden, macht den Aufbau eines Äquivalents zu ImageNet für Zeitserien schwierig. Während Deep Learning unter Verwendung von Zeitreihendaten in vergangenen Studien bereits erfolgreich in verschiedenen Kontexten angewendet wurde, ist ihr Umfang in der Regel auf ihr spezifisches Anwendungsgebiet beschränkt und wird nicht immer rigoros mit anderen State-of-the-Art-Maschinenlernansätzen verglichen.

In diesem Zusammenhang schlägt die vorliegende Arbeit vor, das Thema der Verwendung von Deep Learning für die Klassifizierung von Zeitreihen zu erforschen, welches eines der am häufigsten auftretenden maschinellen Lernprobleme in Ubiquitous-Computing-Anwendungen darstellt. Es wird insbesondere versucht, Antworten auf die foldgenden zwei Fragen zu liefern, die in der Literatur noch nicht vollständig behandelt wurden: 1. Ist es vorteilhaft, Deep Learning für die Zeitreihenklassifizierung gegenüber anderen traditionellen maschinellen Lernansätzen zu verwenden, wenn die Daten begrenzt oder knapp sind? 2. Gibt es eine Möglichkeit, das Problem der Datenknappheit zu umgehen, um die Leistung von DNNs für die Zeitreihenklassifikation zu verbessern? Die Arbeit ist wie folgt strukturiert: Nach einer Einleitung, die den Kontext detaillierter darstellt und Beispiele liefert, die die Schwierigkeiten bei der Anwendung von Deep Learning in der Praxis illustrieren, werden die zwei Kernfragen in jeweils eigenen Kapiteln genauer untersucht.

Der erste Teil der Arbeit (Kapitel 2) untersucht die erste der beiden oben genannten Fragen im Kontext der sensorbasierten Human Activity Recognition (HAR). Sensorbasierte HAR hat sich aufgrund der zahlreichen Anwendungsmöglichkeiten im realen Leben, der Erschwinglichkeit und der weiten Verbreitung von bewegungsbasierten Sensoren sowie der Einfachheit der Datenannotation, die zu relativ großen Datenmengen geführt hat, als die populärste Anwendung des Ubiquitous Computing etabliert. Dieses Kapitel konzentriert sich speziell auf die Frage, wie man geeignete Merkmalsrepräsentationen der Daten für HAR erhält. Die sensorgestützte HAR-Literatur zu diesem Thema ist zwar reichlich vorhanden, aber bisher nur verstreut aufzufinden und es gibt kaum Bemühungen, die Leistungen der verschiedenen Ansätze auf einer fairen Basis zu vergleichen. In diesem Kapitel wird eine vergleichende Studie zwischen verschiedenen State-of-the-Art-Merkmalsextraktionsansätzen - überwacht oder unüberwacht, mit Schwerpunkt auf Feature-Engineering oder Feature Learning mit DNNs - detailliert beschrieben. Ein Evaluierungsrahmen, der einen strengen Vergleich ermöglicht, wird zunächst definiert und zur Durchführung umfangreicher Experimente an zwei sensorbasierten HAR-Benchmark-Datensätzen verwendet: *OPPORTUNITY* und *UniMiB-SHAR*. Die Ergebnisse heben drei Hauptphänomene hervor: die überlegenheit von überwachten Feature-Learning-Ansätzen gegenüber unbeaufsichtigten, die Dominanz von Methoden, die Deep Learning zum Lernen von Features verwenden, gegenüber solchen, die sich auf manuelles Feature-Engineering in allen getesteten Konfigurationen verlassen, und die Effektivität von hybriden DNN-Modellen, die convolutional und recurrent Schichten kombinieren. Die Studie validiert daher die Effektivität von Deep Learning für die Zeitreihenklassifikation im Kontext von sensorbasiertem HAR.

Der zweite Teil dieser Arbeit (Kapitel 3) konzentriert sich auf *transfer learning* für Zeitreihendaten, um die Probleme der Datenknappheit zu umgehen und die Leistung von DNNs für die Zeitreihenklassifikation zu verbessern. Transfer Lerning hat sich als State-of-the-Art Ansatz etabliert, insbesondere wenn es um Bildmodalitäten geht, da es bewiesen wurde, dass DNNs mit der Methodik bessere Klassifizierungsergebnisse erzielen können als ohne. Zeitreihen Transfer Learning ist jedoch noch relativ unerforscht, da weniger Zeitseriendaten zur Verfügung stehen und es große Unterschiede in den Datenformaten gibt, je nachdem, welche Sensoren für die Datenerfassung verwendet wurden. In der Literatur wurden mehrere Transfermethoden vorgeschlagen, aber ihr Umfang ist in der Regel entweder auf bestimmte Anwendungsbereiche, auf strenge ähnlichkeitsbedingungen zwischen dem Quell- und dem Zielgebiet oder auf einkanalige Zeitreihendaten beschränkt. Im Rahmen dieser Arbeit wurde ein neuer Zeitreihen Transfer Learning Ansatz entwickelt, der diese Probleme adressiert. Es wird vorgeschlagen, die Klassifizierung der Sensormodalität als Hilfsaufgabe zu verwenden, um allgemeine übertragbare Zeitserienmerkmale zu lernen. Zeitseriendatensätze, die sich auf verschiedene Anwendungen des Ubiquitous Computing beziehen, werden zunächst aggregiert, um eine Quelldomäne zu bilden. Ein DNN, das einkanalige Daten verarbeitet (sDNN), wird trainiert, um Sensormodalitäten zu erkennen, und seine Gewichte werden dann auf eine DNN-Architektur übertragen, die mehrkanalige Zeitreihen (mDNN) in der Zieldomäne verarbeitet. Das mDNN wird schließlich auf der Zieldomäne feinabgestimmt, um das Zielproblem zu lösen. Dieser Prozess kann auf jede Zieldomäne mit Mehrkanal-Zeitreihendaten angewendet werden, unabhängig davon, wie viele Kanäle verwendet wurden, und behebt so die Einschränkungen bestehender Ansätze. Experimente, die für zwei verschiedene Zielanwendungen des Ubiquitous Computing durchgeführt wurden - sensorbasierte HAR und Emotionserkennung - haben gezeigt, dass der vorgeschlagene Transfer-Ansatz eine Verbesserung der Klassifikationsleistung im Vergleich zum Verzicht auf einen Transfer liefert. Diese Ergebnisse weisen auf das große Potenzial des Ansatzes für Anwendungen des Ubiquitous Computing hin, die auf der Klassifizierung von Zeitreihen beruhen.

Table of contents

Chapter 1

Introduction

The past years have seen a tremendous rise in machine learning applications due to multiple converging factors such as the development of computer hardware with increased processing power and data storage capacities, or societal factors like the democratisation of electronic devices - such as smartphones - taking an increasing place in everyone's daily life. Those trends have received an increasing attention from researchers studying how to take leverage of the increasing availability of such devices, leading to the emergence of the research field of *ubiquitous computing* - term firstly coined by Mark Weiser who predicted those trends three decades ago [1].

Ubiquitous computing is a field centred around the study of *wearable devices*, which refers to electronic devices that can easily be carried by its user. It encompasses a large variety of topics such as the design of practical, unobtrusive and powerful wearable devices, the establishment of communication protocols to retrieve their data in optimal conditions, or the processing of the aforementioned data for complex applications requiring some highly-abstract reasoning. It consequently has a significant overlap with various other research fields. One of them is *machine learning* which refers to an ensemble of techniques to train computers using sensor data to perform complex tasks requiring high-level reasoning, and is widely used to create systems able to provide meaningful applications using the collected data by the wearable devices.

Machine learning heavily relies on the availability of data which should be in quantities as large as possible to train models in optimal conditions. For this reason, it has especially benefitted from the development of ubiquitous computing, and more specifically from the explosion in popularity of wearable sensors of all types such as RGB cameras embedded in smartphones or other devices providing physiological or behavioural data from the wearer. The growing availability of data and the increasing simplicity of sharing them all over the world has led to the emergence of more powerful machine learning approaches over time. The most widely known example of those are Artificial Neural Networks (ANNs), which are the cornerstone of the now famous and pervasive *deep learning*. Despite having been discovered more than 50 years ago, ANNs truly started to explode in popularity only a few years ago following the appearance of increasingly powerful computational units which simplified their training process, and after ANNs significantly outperformed the state-of-the-art for RGB image classification in the *ImageNet Large Scale Visual Recognition Challenge 2012* (ILSVRC 2012) [2]. After their initial success, the machine learning research community was swept away by the deep learning hype, in particular in the field of image processing where data are abundant thanks to past efforts for large-scale data collection and annotation such as the *ImageNet* dataset [3]. After a growing number of studies reported performances never attained previously for several key image processing problems like image classification [2, 4], image segmentation [4], object detection in images [5, 6, 7], etc., ANNs have established themselves as the main state-of-the-art approach for machine learning in the field over the past years.

In the light of the achievements obtained by deep learning on image modalities, the machine learning community has naturally drawn its attention to ANNs for the processing of other types of data. The most important one of those are *time-series data* which designate one-dimensional series of data readings acquired successively in time. Time-series data have a paramount importance in ubiquitous computing because of how sensors measuring one-dimensional series of values are commonly used in ubiquitous computing applications. Numerous past works of the literature have shown promising results for ANNs in several application fields of ubiquitous computing such as sensor-based Human Activity Recognition [8, 9, 10]. But the relative scarcity of time-series datasets (compared to image ones) coupled to the large data requirements to properly train an ANN have limited the application of deep learning on time-series in practice. The objective of this thesis is to provide an additional contribution to the scientific field of time-series deep learning by rigorously comparing its performances to other state-of-the-art machine learning methods and exploring approaches to make its practical application easier.

The rest of the Section is structured as follows: Section 1.1 firstly provides more details about the fundamental concepts surrounding the context of this thesis such as ubiquitous computing (Section 1.1.1), time-series classification (Section 1.1.2) and deep learning (Section 1.1.3). Section 1.2 then expands on the motivation behind this thesis and provides two illustrative examples taken from the experience of the author of this thesis. Section 1.3 explicitly states the contribution of this thesis. Finally, Section 1.4 presents the overall layout of the thesis.

1.1 Fundamental concepts

This Section presents a general overview of the fundamental concepts associated with the context in which this thesis takes place. Section 1.1.1 defines the concept of ubiquitous computing in a more detailed way. Section 1.1.2 explains how machine learning can be applied to ubiquitous computing applications. Finally, Section 1.1.3 provides more details on deep learning - i.e. machine learning with deep ANNs - which supplanted traditional machine learning in many application fields.

1.1.1 Ubiquitous computing

Past years have seen notable technological progress with the explosion in numbers of increasingly powerful, small computers and other smart devices. A prime example illustrating this phenomenon is the constantly increasing popularity and pervasiveness of smartphones. Invented in 1992 by IBM (USA) and popularised to the general public with the release of the first iPhone (Apple Inc., USA) in 2007, smartphones have continuously evolved to provide not only an increasing amount of services, but also of portable sensors. It is now estimated that 3.5 billion people in the world own a smartphone as of 2020, representing a reach of 45.04% of the world population less than three decades after their invention[1].

The remarkably fast spread of increasingly complex and powerful devices is often seen as a consequence of *Moore's law*, which refers to an observation made in 1965 by the then CEO of Intel Gordon Moore who predicted that the number of transistors in an integrated circuit would double every two years, leading to an exponential increase in computational power [11]. Initially estimated to last for only one decade, this trend has remained true until today. While Moore's law validity will necessarily come to an end at some point, experts have not been able to accurately predict when it would happen, with the current estimations placing it somewhere in the upcoming decade[2].

The implications of Moore's law on technological advances and their associated societal changes were understood fairly early on, with the American computer scientist Mark Weiser introducing for the first time the term ubiquitous computing to refer to computers becoming pervasive in everyone's daily life [1] in 1988. Later on, Weiser specified his vision by introducing four fundamental principles defining goals for ubiquitous-computing-related applications [12]:

1. Computers should help their users.

2. While providing their assistance, computers should be quiet and invisible.

3. Computers should "extend the unconscious" of their users, by helping them to make decisions intuitively.

4. Technology should create calm.

Over time, a community aggregated to work on the development of systems following Weiser's four founding principles. The *ubiquitous computing* research area nowadays includes a very wide array of fields such as hardware development to obtain increasingly small and performing sensors, science of design to develop unobtrusive and user-friendly devices, communication and network analysis to develop protocols and methods allowing better and more reliable data transmission

---

[1]Statistics taken from https://www.statista.com/statistics/330695/number-of-smartphone-users-worldwide/ (last accessed on 24/05/2021)

[2]Information taken from https://www.androidauthority.com/moores-law-smartphones-1088760/ (last accessed on 24/05/2021)

or data analysis and machine learning to detect patterns in the data obtained from the wearable devices.

Ubiquitous computing has in particular very close connections with artificial intelligence, which refers to the science of training computers to perform complex tasks, and of which data science and machine learning are sub-fields. Weiser's first and third principles both suggest that computers should assist their users in their decision making, which most of the time involves highly-abstract reasoning. The development of an ubiquitous computing system therefore requires machines to be able to understand and extend such reasoning, which can be provided by machine learning techniques. Since the latter rely on large quantities of data to train the mathematical models required to achieve this objective, the recent expansion of ubiquitous computing has been seen as an opportunity by the machine learning community to develop new means of getting data via wearable devices, leading to an explosion in the number of intelligent systems for many applications such as health monitoring [13], interactive learning systems [14], and assisted living systems for vulnerable people [15].

1.1.2 Machine learning and time-series classification

Machine learning refers to the study of mathematical algorithms which can be used to teach computers to perform complex tasks usually requiring highly-abstract reasoning to be solved. The fundamental way machine learning approaches this goal is by analysing data related to the task considered to train a mathematical model. Once learned from the data, such model is then given to the machine to be re-used on "unseen" real-life data, i.e. data different from the training one used previously to train the model (also referred to as *training data*). It should be noted that machine learning is notably reliant on large quantities of data to work properly, since more of them increases the likelihood that the trained model will learn proper assumptions while generalising well on "unseen" data (which is often referred to as the bias-variance trade-off [16]). Initially evoked for the first time by the American computer scientist A. L. Samuel in 1959 [17], machine learning has become increasingly prevalent over the past decades due to its important overlap with other rising fields of study such as algorithmic, statistics, computer science, data analysis or mathematical optimisation, and due to the large range of applications it could solve. It is for instance widely used in ubiquitous-computing-related studies as a means to provide computers with the "intelligence" required to assist their users in making decisions, thus fulfilling Weiser's first and fourth principles.

Machine learning approaches can be classified into several categories depending on which type of data they require to properly train their models, and how they use them. Three main families of machine learning approaches are usually distinguished:

- **Supervised learning** which relies on using data annotated with *labels* indicating the desired model output for each example of the dataset.

16

- **Unsupervised learning** which attempts to detect patterns in the data without using any labelling information.

- **Semi-supervised learning** which lies in-between supervised and unsupervised learning and attempts to train models using incompletely labelled datasets.

The task of acquiring labels to annotate data - while appearing simple - can prove to be very complicated in real-life due to multiple reasons ranging from labels simply being difficult to obtain (e.g. wearable-emotion recognition described in Section 1.2.2) to the quantity of data being too large to annotate in a reasonable amount of time or resources (e.g. the 14 million images of the *ImageNet* dataset [3]). While labels are not needed in an unsupervised learning context, supervised learning has remained the most widely used category of machine learning approaches until now because of the notably better performances it has obtained compared to semi-supervised or unsupervised learning techniques in most application domains.

When a dataset and its associated labels are available, supervised learning defines and uses a mathematical framework to solve a specific problem for a particular application. Most supervised learning methods do this by translating the problem either into a *regression* or *classification* problem, where regression approaches attempt to train a model to associate its inputs with a specific output value, while classification ones aim at obtaining models able to associate their input data with categorical outputs. Regression and classification approaches are fairly similar in terms of solving procedures or available algorithms. Both aim at approximating a function $\phi : x \rightarrow y$ which maps input data samples x to continuous and discrete labels y, respectively. This is done by computing *features* which refer to values computed on the input data that can be used to properly represent them in an abstract way for the considered problem to solve. Features allow to associate each data sample x with a *feature vector* $\mathbf{f}(\mathbf{x}) = \{f_1(x), f_2(x), ..., f_n(x)\} \in \mathcal{R}^n$ where $n \in \mathcal{N}^*$ is the number of computed features. A mathematical model is then trained in the *feature space* $\mathcal{R}^n$ to match each feature vector $\mathbf{f}(\mathbf{x})$ with its associated label y.

In practice, regression and classification problems however differ in terms of difficulty, with classification models usually being easier to train than regression ones. While any machine learning approach requires large quantities of training data and associated labels, regression approaches tend to need more of them than classification in order to precisely approximate their continuous targets. Classification has therefore become the preponderant framework in most machine learning applications.

The reliance of machine learning on large quantities of available data had the consequence of splitting the research community depending on which sensor modalities they use to provide input data for their models. Machine learning approaches remain the same independently of what type of data is used in the training set. In practice however, it has been observed that the relevance of the trained models increases substantially the more data is available. As a consequence, a divide has effectively appeared over the past decade between researchers working with image modalities - where the quantity of available data is plentiful due to the pervasiveness of cameras and some initiatives to build very large scale datasets like *ImageNet* [3] - and those working with other sensor modalities. Ubiquitous computing researchers tend to fall into the second category as the intrusiveness (and sometimes obtrusiveness) of cameras could be considered as a contradiction of Weiser's second principle of "computers being invisible to the user". As a result, ubiquitous computing applications have favoured the use of wearable sensors providing data values sequentially in time, also commonly referred to as *time-series data*.

In this context, time-series classification has become an important topic for sensor-based applications, with abundant works in the past literature trying to propose high performing classification approaches in many application fields such as Human Activity Recognition, sensor-based emotion and pain recognition (respectively discussed in Sections 2, 1.2.2 and 1.2.3). Mirroring the trends in the image processing research community, time-series classification has in particular been strongly impacted by the rise of deep learning, which has established itself as the new baseline approach over the past years.

1.1.3 Deep learning

Deep learning is a term introduced by the American artificial learning professor Rina Dechter in 1986 [18] to refer to machine learning using deep *Artificial Neural Networks* (ANNs).

ANNs are a class of mathematical models whose principles are loosely based on how biological neurons in the human brain work. They consist of a set of interconnected *artificial neurons*, where each artificial neuron is a very simple non-linear computational unit as shown in Figure 1.1. Each neuron takes a multidimensional input $\mathbf{x} = \{x_1, x_2, ..., x_n\} \in \mathcal{R}^n$ with $n \in \mathcal{N}^*$ and outputs a single value $y \in \mathcal{R}$ using the following equation:

$$y = \sigma(\sum_{k=1}^{n} w_k x_k) + b$$

where σ is a non-linear function referred to as *activation function*, $\forall k \in \{1, 2, ..., n\}, w_k \in \mathcal{R}$ are internal parameters referred to as *neural weights* and $b \in \mathcal{R}$ is an offset parameter called *neural bias*.

In an ANN, artificial neurons are organised in a layer-wise structure with the outputs of the neurons of one layer being used as inputs of the neurons of the next layer as shown in Figure 1.2. A layer of an ANN with $n_{in} \in \mathcal{N}^*$ inputs and $n_{out} \in \mathcal{N}^*$ outputs can therefore be mathematically represented by the formula:

$$\mathbf{y} = \sigma(\mathbf{W}\mathbf{x} + \mathbf{b})$$

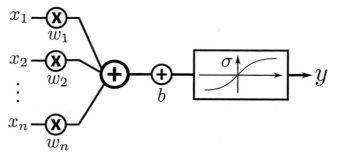

Figure 1.1: Graph of an artificial neuron: $n \in \mathcal{N}^*$ inputs $\{x_1, x_2, ..., x_n\} \in \mathcal{R}^n$ are multiplied by n weights $\{w_1, w_2, ..., w_n\} \in \mathcal{R}^n$, summed together, added to a bias $b \in \mathcal{R}$ and then sent throught a non-linear function σ to provide an output value $y \in \mathcal{R}$.

where $\mathbf{y} \in \mathcal{R}^{n_{out}}$ is the vector of the layer neural outputs, $\mathbf{x} \in \mathcal{R}^{n_{in}}$ is the vector of the layer inputs, $\mathbf{W} \in \mathcal{R}^{n_{out} \times n_{in}}$ is the matrix of weights connecting the neurons to the ones of the previous layer and $\mathbf{b} \in \mathcal{R}^{n_{out}}$ is the vector containing the biases of the neurons of the layer. Similarly, an ANN stacking $N \in \mathcal{N}^*$ layers containing $n^{(l)} \in \mathcal{N}^*$ neurons each (for $1 \leq l \leq N$) can be mathematically represented as a series of composite activation functions:

$$\mathbf{y}^{(l)} = \begin{cases} \sigma(\mathbf{W}^{(l)}\mathbf{x} + \mathbf{b}^{(l)}) & \text{if } l = 1 \\ \sigma(\mathbf{W}^{(l)}\mathbf{y}^{(l-1)} + \mathbf{b}^{(l)}) & \text{if } 2 \leq l \leq N \end{cases}$$

where $\mathbf{y}^{(l)} \in \mathcal{R}^{n^{(l)}}$, $\mathbf{W}^{(l)} \in \mathcal{R}^{n^{(l)} \times n^{(l-1)}}$, $\mathbf{b}^{(l)} \in \mathcal{R}^{n^{(l)}}$ respectively refer to the output, weight matrix and biases of layer $l \in \{1, 2, ..., N\}$, and x to the input of the network.

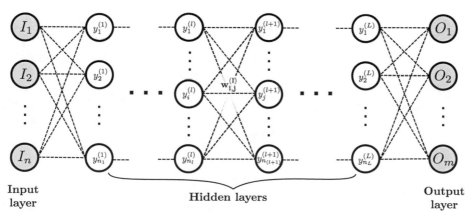

Input layer

Hidden layers

Output layer

Figure 1.2: Example of an artificial neural network with $n \in \mathcal{N}^*$ inputs, $m \in \mathcal{N}^*$ outputs and $L \in \mathcal{N}^*$ layers. Each layer l has $n_l \in \mathcal{N}^*$ neurons (for $1 \leqslant l \leqslant L$). $y_i^{(l)}$ and $w_{i,j}^{(l)}$ respectively designate the output of the ith neuron in the lth layer and the weight connecting the ith neuron on layer l to the jth neuron of layer $l + 1$.

The first and last layers of an ANN are respectively called *input* and *output layers*, while intermediate ones are referred to as *hidden layers*. An ANN is considered to be *deep* as long as it has at least two hidden layers, and is in that case referred to as *Deep Neural Network* (DNN). ANNs can be used for regression or classification purposes by adapting the size and activation functions of their output layer. For classification in particular, the common practice consists of setting the number of output neurons to the number of classes and using a *softmax* activation function [19]. Each neuron of a softmax output layer yields a value between 0 and 1 and the sum of all softmax outputs is equal to 1. The output of one softmax neuron can therefore be assimilated to a probability score of the ANN input data being associated to its corresponding class.

The *training of an ANN* (or DNN) refers to the process of fine-tuning the internal parameters of the model - weights and biases of the neurons of all layers - so that it can produce the desired outputs on its output layer. Neural weights and biases are usually initialised to values following an initialisation scheme that proved its effectiveness in practice, such as the *Glorot* initialisation strategy [20] which picks values at random in an interval whose boundaries depend on the sizes of the current and next layers for each neuron. Weights and biases are then iteratively updated during the training process. This is performed by firstly defining a *loss function* $\mathcal{L}$ which computes the errors between the expected and neural outputs, and then minimising the loss function using a mathematical optimisation approach. For ANNs, the most commonly used method is the *gradient descent approach* which consists in iteratively updating each internal parameter $\theta \in \mathcal{R}$ of a given ANN (i.e. weight or bias) in the opposite direction of the derivative of the loss function with respect to θ, i.e.

$$\forall \theta \,, \, \theta \leftarrow \theta - \lambda \frac{\partial \mathcal{L}}{\partial \theta}(x)$$

where $\lambda \in \mathcal{R}^{+*}$ is a parameter to control the speed of updates called *learning rate* and $x \in \mathcal{R}^n$ an input example of the training set. The updating process is repeated for all samples x of the training set to complete one *epoch*. For ANNs, $\frac{\partial \mathcal{L}}{\partial \theta}(x)$ can only be directly computed if θ is a parameter belonging to the output layer by using the chain rule of derivation. The updates to the parameters belonging to the other layers are performed by using the *backpropagation algorithm* [21] which back-propagates the loss to the neurons of the previous layers using the chain rule of derivation. More in details, using the following notations:

- $N \in \mathcal{N}^*$ number of layers of the ANN

- $n^{(l)} \in \mathcal{N}^*$ number of neurons of layer l (with $1 \leq l \leq N$)

- $\mathcal{L}$ loss function

- σ activation function (assumed to be the same for all neurons of the ANN)

- $w_{ij}^{(l)} \in \mathcal{R}$ weight between the ith neuron of layer $l-1$ and the jth neuron of layer l (with $2 \leq l \leq N$)

- $y_j^{(l)} \in \mathcal{R}$ output of the jth neuron of layer l

- $b_j^{(l)} \in \mathcal{R}$ bias of the jth neuron of layer l

- $s_j^{(l)} \in \mathcal{R}$ weighted sum of inputs of the jth neuron of layer l, i.e. $y_j^{(l)} = \sigma(s_j^{(l)} + b_j^{(l)})$

it can be shown that

$$\frac{\partial \mathcal{L}}{\partial w_{ij}^{(l)}}(x) = s_i^{(l-1)} \delta_j^{(l)}$$

with

$$\delta_j^{(l)} = \begin{cases} \frac{\partial \sigma(s_j^{(l)})}{\partial s_j^{(l)}} \frac{\partial \mathcal{L}}{\partial y_j^{(l)}}(x) & \text{if } l = N \\ \frac{\partial \sigma(s_j^{(l)})}{\partial s_j^{(l)}} \sum_{k=1}^{n^{(l)}} w_{jk} \delta_k^{(l+1)} & \text{otherwise.} \end{cases}$$

Neural biases are updated in a similar way as weights by the backpropagation algorithm by considering them as a neural weight associated with a constant input of 1.

ANNs are fairly old models whose origins are usually reported to go back as far as 1943, when the American scientists Warren McCulloch and Walter Pitts proposed a simplified version of the artificial neuron called Threshold Logic Unit [22]. This idea was later on expanded by various researchers such as the American psychologist F. Rosenblatt who introduced the *perceptron* model in 1958 [23] which served as a basis for the current modelling of artificial neurons, or the Ukrainian mathematician A. Ivakhnenko who was the first to propose a network structure featuring several layers in 1967 [24]. DNNs were however dismissed for a long time because they were considered as too complex to train properly. Methods to train DNNs based on gradient descent approaches had been found as early as 1974 [25] but could not be applied in practice due to high complexity caused by the high number of parameters in an ANN, associated with hardware-related limitations. It is only during the last decade that the training of ANNs - and more specifically DNNs - has become practical with researches highlighting the possibility to take leverage of high computational power units such as Graphics Processing Units (GPUs) to properly apply the backpropagation algorithm to large DNNs [26]. In the wake of those findings, deep learning started to yield state-of-the-art performances largely outperforming other traditional machine learning approaches, in particular in the field of image processing. The beginning of the deep learning hype is considered to coincide with the DNN *AlexNet* winning the ImageNet Large Scale Visual Recognition Challenge in 2012 (ILSVRC2012) by a very large margin over other machine learning methods [2]. Since then, DNNs have progressively established themselves as the main machine learning approach when image modalities are involved, and their use is now generalising to other types of modalities too, including time-series.

In the wake of the popularisation of deep learning, the reasons for the success and remarkable performances of DNNs have been thoroughly investigated in past researches. Because of the complexity of the mathematical concepts surrounding such models (analysis of complex composite functions), deep learning research has been notably lacking a solid mathematical framework until now. As a result, most works in the literature have remained fairly application-oriented so far. They have, however, highlighted a few key aspects of DNNs:

- **Strong representative power:** in 1989, the *Universal Approximation Theorem* was demonstrated [27], which states that any basic ANN with a single hidden layer containing an arbitrarily large (but finite) number of neurons can approximate any continuous function taking its input values on compact subsets of $\mathcal{R}^n$, under the assumption that the activation function is not polynomial. The implications of such findings are very impactful as they suggest that ANNs could be theoretically used to solve a very large variety of problems. In practice, it was shown that the number of neurons required for a single-hidden layer ANN to work properly might be too large to be practical depending on the complexity of the function to approximate [28]. Past works have nevertheless shown that using DNNs instead of shallow models could still yield good performances, largely outperforming traditional machine learning approaches in several application domains - in particular related to image processing - such as image classification [2, 7] and object detection [5, 4, 7].

- **Flexibility and modularity:** past researches showed that the traditional architecture of DNNs could be altered to better fit some specific application problems without fundamentally changing the mathematical background behind deep learning (gradient-descent-based training procedure especially). This has in particular led to the emergence of Convolutional Neural Networks (CNNs) pioneered by Kunihiko Fukushima [29] and Yann LeCun [30] for image-based applications, or of Recurrent Neural Networks (RNNs) whose first successful practical application was reported for speech recognition by Sepp Hochreiter [31]. More details about both architectures will be reported in Section 2.3.2. Alterations to the traditional DNN structure explored in the past literature have also included combinations of different types of DNNs [2, 8].

- **Feature learning:** a study carried out by Matthew Zeiler in 2013 [32] highlighted an interesting property of CNNs by showing that each neuron in the convolutional layers of the *AlexNet* model trained for image classification on *ImageNet* [2] was detecting a specific visual pattern whose complexity increased the deeper the layer was (e.g. straight lines or edges for neurons in the first layers, specific object parts for neurons of the deeper layers). Such findings suggest that each neuron learns a specific feature on the input data whose level of abstraction is higher the deeper the layer this neuron belongs to is. Other studies corroborated such behaviour, showing in particular that it was also observed for other types of DNNs for applications other than image classification such as speech recognition from audio data [33]. As a result, deep learning has progressively taken the place of old traditional approaches relying on asking domain experts to suggest features for a specific classification problem in such application fields.

- **Scalability with big data:** DNNs have shown to benefit from a large number of training examples more than other traditional machine learning models for regression or classification. Traditional approaches such as Support Vector Machines (SVM) [34] or Random Forests (RF) [35] for instance both have a training complexity at least quadratic with their number of training examples, and therefore cannot be trained under reasonable amounts of time on large datasets in practice. The compatibility of deep learning to the current era of big data - where large amounts of data are increasingly easily shared and stored - has contributed to the rise of its popularity over the past years.

Despite the current overwhelming popularity of DNNs in the machine learning community, the application of deep learning still remains confronted with some difficulties in practice, like the need for powerful computational resources to train complex models on large datasets in a reasonable amount of time (e.g. the DNN *VGG-Net* trained for ILSVRC2014 took between two to three consecutive weeks to be trained on four NVIDIA Titan Black GPUs [36]). The lack of rigorous mathematical framework surrounding DNNs also causes some deep learning aspects to still remain obscure as of today. Some topics such as how to optimise DNNs hyper-parameters (e.g. number of layers, number of neurons per layer, choice of the optimiser and learning rate, etc.) [37, 38, 39] or to interpret the decisions process of a trained DNN [40, 41] still remain active nowadays, especially in the image processing research field where data are more abundant.

1.2 Motivation

This section provides more details on the motivation of the thesis with regards to the context described in Section 1.1. Section 1.2.1 defines the problems that the thesis attempts to address. Sections 1.2.2 and 1.2.3 provide two practical examples - respectively about sensor-based emotion recognition and sensor-based pain recognition - to illustrate the difficulties raised in the previous Section. Section 1.3 lists the main contributions of this thesis and explains how they address the problems. Finally, Section 1.4 provides more details about the structure of the thesis.

1.2.1 Context

Despite promising results obtained in many application fields of ubiquitous computing, deep learning methods remain difficult to apply to time-series data properly. Two reasons mainly explain this phenomenon.

The first reason is that in order to be trained properly, DNNs tend to require an even larger amount of data than other machine learning models. DNNs are models which typically contain a high number of internal trainable parameters - in that case, neural weights and biases. For instance, the matrix of weights between two

23

consecutive fully-connected layers - which are the most basic type of layers for DNNs - contain $n \times m$ elements, where n and m are the respective sizes of both layers. The total number of parameters of one DNN therefore quickly grows as more layers are stacked or as their size is increased. This often happens in practice since a DNN without enough layers or neurons can lead to a model underfitting on its training set [42]. At the time of writing of this thesis, no rigorously demonstrated rule on what would be the minimum amount of data required to train a machine learning model with $N \in \mathbf{N}^*$ parameters has been found. But several rules of the thumb are being used in practice by machine learning researchers, such as "use at least N^2 training examples" or "use between $20 \times N$ and $30 \times N$ training examples"[3]. With N being very high for DNNs in general, such criteria can often be difficult to fulfil [28] (e.g. the famous image processing *AlexNet* DNN [2], which arguably initiated the hype for deep learning in 2012, contains more than 62 million parameters!).

The second reason is the relative scarcity of time-series data, especially when compared to image data. Acquiring time-series data has been made significantly easier by the progress in ubiquitous computing over the past years. But despite this, obtaining a large scale dataset for a specific application remains very costly in terms of time and resources, especially if such a dataset needs to be annotated to be used for supervised learning approaches. In addition to this, the fact that some wearable devices can be considered as recording personal medical data (e.g. ElectroCardioGram (ECG), ElectroEncephaloGram (EEG), ...) [43] adds some obstacles related to data privacy (e.g. constraints in acquiring and sharing the data, reluctance to provide the data, ...). As a result, the vast majority of the many datasets publicly available for diverse applications of ubiquitous computing are very small. Since such data are also usually acquired with different wearable devices, the data format can differ a lot, even for datasets that relate to the same application field and contain the same sensor modalities. For this reason, it becomes very difficult to fuse many small time-series datasets to form a large benchmark and meet the strong constraints on the dataset size imposed by DNNs (similarly to what was partially done for images with *ImageNet*).

Many pieces of work exploring solutions to help the training of DNNs when data are scarce have been proposed for image modalities. A large number of them are based on *transfer learning* [44], a sub-field of machine learning that includes techniques attempting to learn knowledge on some domain - referred to as *source* -, and then transferring it to improve the performances of a main task on another - *target* - domain. Transfer learning for DNNs - also referred to as *deep transfer learning* - consists of a transfer of weights and biases: a DNN is firstly trained on the source domain, setting weights and biases to optimal values for the source task. They are then transferred to initialise another similar DNN model whose purpose is to solve the target task. This DNN is then finally fine-tuned on the target domain. Deep transfer learning has yielded consistent improvements in performances compared to the case when it is not used when image modali-

---

[3]Taken from `https://www.researchgate.net/post/What_is_the_minimum_sample_size_required_to_train_a_Deep_Learning_model-CNN` (last accessed on 24/05/2021)

ties are involved, to the point where using image classification on *ImageNet* as source task has become state-of-the-art for a large variety of target tasks [45, 46, 47].

The situation surrounding the usage of DNNs is much less clear when it comes to the processing of time-series. Firstly, the dominance of deep feature learning is not as established as for image modalities. Many past pieces of work have hinted that DNNs could yield promising performances in some applications of ubiquitous computing, but those are often not compared to other feature extraction approaches in a fair way. Secondly, the literature remains much more scarce when it comes to deep transfer learning for time-series. No transfer learning approach with a general scope has been proposed so far for multi-channel (also referred to as multimodal) time-series data, partially due to the lack of an equivalent of *ImageNet*. The existing time-series transfer learning approaches have usually their scope either restricted by assumptions of similarity between source and target domains (e.g. same type of data, same classes to be recognised, etc.) [48, 49, 50], or limited by the fact that they can be applied only on single-channel (unimodal) time-series [51]. It is in this context that this thesis proposes to investigate deep learning and deep transfer learning applied to classification problems using time-series data. In particular, it proposes contributions to explore the current aforementioned limitations of the literature, and answer the two following questions:

Superiority of deep learning to traditional machine learning: Considering the difficulty to train deep learning models properly, is there really a benefit to use them for time-series classification as opposed to other traditional machine learning models?

Enhancing deep feature learning on time-series data with transfer learning: Is it possible to propose a time-series transfer learning approach with a general scope to make the training of DNNs easier and improve their performances?

Before describing the contents of this thesis in more details, the next two subsections provide examples highlighting the difficulties of applying DNNs to time-series classification in practice. Both examples are taken from various research projects linked to two very different application fields of ubiquitous computing (sensor-based emotion recognition and pain recognition) that the author of this thesis was involved in.

1.2.2 Example 1: *ELISE* - sensor-based emotion recognition

The following subsections describes the first example illustrating the difficulties to apply DNNs on time-series data in practice. Experimental results reported in this Section were carried out in the frame of the research project *ELISE* funded by the German Ministry of Education and Research (referred to as BMBF; grant number: 16SV7512) and reported in two conference publications (ITIB 2018 [52], IEEE BIBE 2018 [53]). The project aimed at obtaining a system for automatic recognition of some specific emotional states (happiness, frustration, boredom) using physiological data as input (skin Temperature, EEG, EOG, ECG, GSR). Section 1.2.2 firstly provides an overview of the research field of sensor-based emotion recognition and its challenges. Section 1.2.2 then describes the *ELISE* project itself in more details. Section 1.2.2 describes the dataset acquired in the frame of the *ELISE* project. Section 1.2.2 presents experiments and results carried out in the frame of this project. Section 1.2.2 finally performs an overall overview of the project and proposes future steps to be carried out to expand on the obtained results.

Definition and challenges

Sensor-based emotion recognition is a relatively young research field which has gained popularity with the progress in the miniaturisation of physiological sensors such as ElectroEncephaloGram (EEG), Galvanic Skin Response (GSR) or ElectroOcculoGram (EOG). Its goal is to propose methods to obtain a system which can automatically provide an estimation of the emotional state of one subject based on the analysis of the data coming from sensor devices worn by the subject. It has several potential practical applications such as the design of enhanced learning systems which would take into account the current affect of the student to adapt its answers and ways to teach accordingly [14, 52, 53], or the design of advanced automatic recommendation systems, for instance for music suggestion [54].

The goal of automatically recognising emotions using sensor data is not new in itself and has always been an important component of the research field of *affective computing*, which aims at teaching machines to recognise human affect and uses machine learning techniques to reach this goal [55]. From a machine learning point of view, emotion recognition can be abstracted as a classification problem. Each emotional state to be recognised is defined as one class. A classification model taking sensor data as input is then trained to correctly match the data to their relevant class - most of the time using supervised learning techniques due to their tendency to achieve better results than either semi-supervised or unsupervised ones.

For a long time, state-of-the-art approaches for emotion recognition had mostly relied on the analysis of facial expressions of the subjects captured by video modalities (e.g. RGB cameras). The predominance of such video-based approaches could be explained by the popularity of the *Basic Emotions* theory proposed by the American psychologist P. Ekman in order to scientifically define emotions [56]. In his research works, Ekman identified six "universal emotions" which could be recognised through analysis of the facial expressions of an individual regardless of their cultural background: happiness, sadness, fear, disgust, anger, surprise. This theory served as a basis for many other past work also hypothesising that emotions could be described as discrete categories and recognised via the analysis of facial expressions. Examples of such pieces of work include Plutchik's *Wheel of Emotions* [57] which proposes to associate each of the six basic Ekman emotions to an antagonistic one, leading to 8 basic emotions split into positive and negative subsets (happiness, anger, trust and anticipation opposed to sadness, fear, disgust and surprise). To allow his model to modelise more complex emotional states,

26

Plutchik also proposed emotions obtained after merging non-antagonist basic ones (e.g. happiness + anticipation = optimism).

The use of video modalities to detect emotions via analysis of facial expressions has however receded over the past years because of multiple concurrent factors. The first and most important one is the loss of popularity of all the aforementioned emotion modelisation approaches - which could be referred to as *categorical approaches* - in favour of an alternative approach proposed by J. A. Russell, called the *Circumplex Model of Affect* [58]. To define emotions, Russell based his work on semantic studies analysing verbal emotional expressions instead of facial expression analysis. This led him to propose the decomposition of a specific emotional state along several components (i.e. axes), of which the two most widely used are *arousal* - level of excitement - and *valence* - level of pleasantness. Not only does this model allow one to conveniently characterise any emotional state (e.g. happiness = high valence and arousal, anger = high arousal and low valence, etc.), it can also handle transitions between emotions in a better way than categorical approaches. One of the important corollaries implied by Russell's findings states that the analysis of facial emotions is not required to properly detect emotions, which led researchers to investigate modalities other than image-based ones. This was confirmed by numerous studies which showed strong correlations between levels of arousal and valence and physiological features coming from modalities such as GSR [59, 60] or EEG [61]. The second factor explaining the loss of popularity of video-based emotion recognition techniques is related to practical considerations: obtaining clean images of the face of a subject requires constraining experimental setups (e.g. proper alignment of the face with the camera, monitoring of proper lighting conditions, etc.). Those difficulties added to the intrusiveness of video-based sensors led emotion recognition researchers to investigate other methods based on using wearable physiological sensors.

The growing number of studies reporting encouraging results for sensor-based emotion recognition highlights the increasing popularity of this topic. But several obstacles remain which prevent obtaining recognition results good enough for a large scale application. The first one is the overall scarcity of available emotion-related data. This phenomenon has two main causes:

- The difficulty to design an experimental protocol which would reliably induce specific emotional states. Past works have attempted to propose induction setups for some specific emotions (e.g. classical music and positive text reading for happiness [62], peg-turning game for boredom [63], Wisconsin sorting card test for frustration [64], etc.). However, the reproducibility of such results is not granted depending on the tested subjects (as discussed in Section 1.2.2).

- The difficulty to reliably annotate emotion-related data. If some past studies have attempted to use external observers to estimate the mood of their subjects based on analysis of facial images [65], the overwhelming majority relies on self-reporting. Exactly characterising one's emotional state remains however a difficult task which can lead to uncertainty in the provided labels (e.g. when asking someone to describe their current emotional state, one might receive vague answers such as "I feel happy overall, maybe also a little bit stressed").

The second obstacle hindering progress in emotion-related research is the high *intra-class variability* which exists in any emotion recognition problem. Two different individuals might have very different ways to react in a specific emotional state both in terms of behaviour (e.g. facial expressions) and physiology (e.g. Heart Rate, EEG, GSR, etc.). As a consequence, obtaining a "universal" emotion classifier which would successfully predict the emotional state of any subject - that we refer to as *subject-independent* classifier - is made more complex [66, 67]. As a result, the current literature in wearable-emotion recognition has mostly focused on obtaining what we refer to as *subject-dependent* models, i.e. classification models trained on the data of one (or more) subject(s) to recognise the emotions of this (or these) subject(s) specifically [68, 69]. While this particular pattern recognition problem is easier to solve than the subject-independent case, its real-life applications are also more narrow since it is generally not possible to obtain good classification performances using a subject-dependent classifier on "unseen" subjects who did not provide data to train the model.

Despite those difficulties, research on the topic of sensor-based emotion recognition continues to be investigated. The following sections give an example of such projects as well as the associated classification results which can be obtained.

ELISE

The *ELISE* project is a BMBF-funded project which ran from February 2016 to February 2019. It was led by the gaming company *Limbic Entertainment* and involved both industrial and academic partners such as Software AG, the chairs of *Wirtschaftsinformatik*, *Mikrosystementwurf* and (the former chair of) *Mustererkennung* of the University of Siegen (Germany) respectively led by Prof. Niehaves, Prof. Brück and Prof. Grzegorzek.

Its main objective was the design of a *Virtual Reality (VR) serious game* to enhance the learning of some specific business processes. In more details, a specific business skill process (e.g. packet management in a post office) was simulated and turned into a game in VR. The subject (learner) was then asked to play the game while successfully completing the different steps of the process (e.g. welcome the client, weigh and measure packages, add stamps, etc.). At the end of the session, detailed statistics and evaluations were provided to the subject to indicate them which steps of the process were done well and which ones could be improved.

In order to further improve the learning experience, an emotion recognition module was integrated to the game to detect the affect of the player in real time and let the game automatically perform micro (e.g. change of background music) and macro-adaptations (e.g. change of the game difficulty) to keep the player engagement as high as possible during the session. Preliminary research in the

Figure 1.3: Example of the use case of the *ELISE* system. A participant is playing the *ELISE* VR game to train for packet management in a post office. A headband with various sensor modalities records physiological data which are used to estimate his current emotional state. The game self-adapts its difficulty based on this estimation.

field of affective computing showed in particular the importance of three specific emotions in a learning context: happiness, frustration and boredom [14]. The detection of boredom might for instance indicate an uninteresting game for the subject due to a too low level of difficulty, while frustration might be a sign that the contrary is happening. Happiness can also be used to measure the player's level of engagement in the game.

A VR game requires the use of a VR head-set to be played, which covers a large part of the subject's face. In this context, the use of image modalities to analyse facial expressions is made impossible. In *ELISE*, it was decided to use physiological signals acquired by sensors placed on the subject's head. To reach this goal, the chair of *Medizinische Informatik und Mikrosystementwurf* of the University of Siegen (Germany) designed a multi-sensor platform recording the following physiological signals [53]:

- **Blood Volume Pulse (BVP):** measure of cardiovascular dynamics by detection of changes in the arterial translucency.

- **Photoplethysmogram (PPG):** measure of the oxygen saturation in blood.

- **Galvanic Skin Response (GSR):** measure of the continuous variation in the electrical characteristics of the skin due to the autonomic nervous system.

- **Temperature:** measure of the temperature of the surface of the skin.

- **Electroencephalography (EEG):** measure of the electrical activity generated by the synchronised activity of neurons in the brain.

- **Electrooculography (EOG):** measures of voltages across the eyes to detect eye movements.

All signals were recorded in real-time at a frequency of $416Hz$ and sent to a receiving station (e.g. smartphone or laptop) via Bluetooth. The multi-sensor platform yielded a total of $S = 9$ data channels.

Data acquisition

A dataset labelled with emotion-related annotations was acquired using the multi-sensor platform described in the previous section. Due to the need to detect very specific emotional states in the *ELISE* project, it was decided to use the categorical approach inspired from Ekman's works for emotion modelisation. Four classes were defined: happiness, frustration, boredom and a final class referred to as "other" gathering all other emotions not specifically relevant to the project.

Emotion induction is a difficult topic, because it is difficult to reliably put a subject in a specific emotional state. While previous works about happiness [62], frustration [64] and boredom [63] induction existed in the literature, preliminary experiments performed in the frame of the project showed that not all of them worked as effectively as previously reported. This gap between reported and observed efficiency is hypothesised to be caused by contextual, contemporary or cultural differences among the subjects of the literature and the *ELISE* study.

For those reasons, it was decided in particular to use a completely different emotion induction experimental protocol for frustration compared to the *Wisconsin card sorting test* introduced in Berg et al. [64], and to slightly modify the one taken from [62] for happiness induction. In addition, the unreliability of the boredom protocol reported in [63] led to the adoption of a second boredom induction session. In the end, the four following protocols were selected:

- **Happiness induction:** inspired by [62], subjects were asked to listen to an extract of the classical song *Delibes (1870): Mazurka aus Coppelia* using headphones, while simultaneously reading vignettes with text describing various cheerful situations on a screen (e.g. "You found a new job, and it is even better than your previous one!", "You won 20 euros in the lottery!", etc.). Each vignette was displayed for 30 seconds and emphasised by an image describing its context (addition compared to the protocol in [62]) as shown in Figure 1.4. The texts of the vignettes used in [62] were slightly modified to describe more contemporary situations.

- **First boredom induction:** inspired by [63], subjects were asked to play a peg-turning game as illustrated in Figure 1.5. They received a single instruction to click a peg displayed on a screen using a mouse. After each click, the peg was rotated clockwise and the subject had to wait for five seconds before performing another click. The whole session lasted for five minutes, without any other specific event happening in-between.

- **Frustration induction:** the subject was asked to play a Flash-based maze game[4] controlled by a mouse, whose goal is to navigate through a labyrinth while avoiding walls and obstacles, as illustrated in Figure 1.6. Subjects were promised a financial reward if they were able to complete a certain amount of levels under a certain time threshold. A wireless mouse plugged to the subject's computer was controlled by the supervisor to make sure the requirement could not be achieved, without the subject knowing. A comparable setup with a rigged mouse was already successfully used in [70].

- **Second boredom induction:** the subject was asked to watch a video about a specific German tax law presented in a neutral and emotionless way, in neutral environment devoid of distraction sources[5].

Figure 1.4: Example of vignette shown to the subject during the happiness induction protocol. The text of the vignette (in German) can be translated as "You got a new job and it is even better than you expected!".

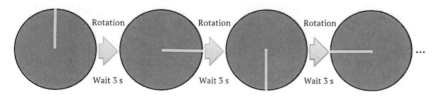

Figure 1.5: Peg-turning game used to induce boredom in the frame of the *ELISE* data acquisition process. The subject was asked to keep clicking on a peg to rotate it 90° clockwise for the five minutes of the protocol. A five-second timer was set between each click.

---

[4]*Frustrabit*: http://www.notdoppler.com/frustrabit.php (last accessed on 03/05/2021)
[5]https://www.youtube.com/watch?v=nhcG8zC7G2o (last accessed on 24/05/2021).

 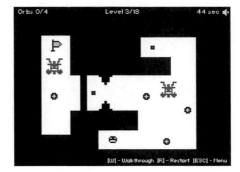

Figure 1.6: Flash-based maze game used to induce frustration in the frame of the *ELISE* data acquisition process. The goal of the game consists of controlling a character with a computer mouse to reach the end of a maze without touching any walls or obstacles. To raise frustration levels, the game was rigged to prevent this from happening by adding a wireless mouse controlled by the supervisor and hidden from the player's view.

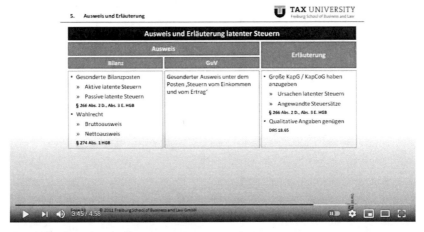

Latente Steuern im Jahresabschluss

Figure 1.7: Screenshot of the Youtube video used for boredom induction in the frame of the *ELISE* data acquisition process. The video describes a specific German tax law (in German).

All aforementioned scenarios were designed to last between four and five minutes. At the end of each one, the subjects were asked to fill out a questionnaire containing two items (shown in Figure 1.8). The first one asked them to indicate on a 5-point scale their subjectively felt intensity of 11 emotions selected by analysing Ekman's and Plutchik's works, as well as specific *ELISE* requirements (fear, enthusiasm, frustration, boredom, curiosity, calmness, sadness, surprise, anger, satisfaction, nervousness). The second item asked subjects to indicate which of those 11 emotions dominated during each quarter of the emotion induction session (with the option to choose none). The answers to this second item were used to label the time-series data obtained from the physiological sensors on a timestamp level.

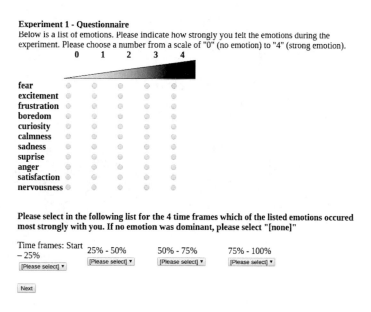

Figure 1.8: Emotion questionnaire used in the frame of the *ELISE* data acquisition session. After each protocol, subjects were asked to fill out one questionnaire to assess 11 different emotions taken from the literature. The first part of the questionnaire asked subjects to rate the intensity of each emotion during the experiment on a 5-point scale. The second part asked them to indicate their dominant emotion during each quarter of the previous protocol.

Using the aforementioned emotion induction scenarios and multi-sensor platform, the labelled data from 15 subjects recruited in the University of Siegen (Germany) were collected (8 male, 7 female, $\mu_{age} = 23.87$ years, $\sigma_{age} = 4.49$ years).

Experiments and results

A standard supervised learning approach was used to train a model to predict emotions by taking one-second frames of data coming from the multi-sensor platform as input. The data acquired from the 15 subjects were labelled with labels for happiness (enthusiasm+satisfaction), frustration (frustration+anger), boredom and other classes.

The most common approach in the literature for the processing of multimodal time-series data using DNNs consists of extracting data frames with a fixed length in time from the original data records, and then send them to the input of the DNN. For this purpose, the original data records were segmented into 1-second data frames using a sliding window approach without overlap, as shown in Figure 1.9. A total of 16,202 frames was obtained after application of the segmentation process with a class distribution provided in Table 1.1.

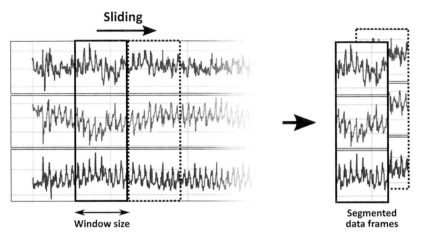

Figure 1.9: Example of segmentation with a non-overlapping sliding window approach on multichannel time-series data records.

Class	Happiness	Frustration	Boredom	Other
Number data frames	3,317	801	3,412	8,672
Dataset proportion (%)	20.47	4.94	21.06	53.53

Table 1.1: Class distribution of the *ELISE* dataset

Two different approaches to train the emotion classifier were tested:

- **Hand-crafted features (HCF):** a traditional approach consisting of manually computing features on each sensor channel of a data frame. A standard normalisation was applied channel-wise on each channel of the input frames before feature extraction. The list of extracted features is provided in Table 1.2 and includes features computed on both time and frequency domains. In total, 270 features were computed on a single data frame. The 270-dimensional feature vectors were then used to train a Soft-margin Support-Vector Machine (SVM) classifier with Radial-Basis Function (RBF) kernel whose parameters were fine-tuned by grid search.

- **DNNs:** an approach attempting to obtain deep learning-based features by training DNN models with a softmax [19] classification layer taking the data frames directly as input. Several types of DNNs were tested including Multi-Layer-Perceptrons (MLP), Convolutional Neural Networks (CNNs), Recurrent Neural Networks (RNNs) with Long-Short-Term Memory (LSTM) cells. All aforementioned models will be described in more details in Section 2.3.2. The hyper-parameters of each model were fine-tuned by trial and error.

Features computed on the time domain	· average · maximum · amplitude · kurtosis · interquartile range · number of peaks	· standard-deviation · minimum · skewness · percentile 25/50/75 · zero-crossing
Features computed on the power spectrum	· standard-deviation · maximum	· average · minimum

Table 1.2: Hand-crafted features computed on each sensor channel of each data frame of the *ELISE* dataset

All models were evaluated using the Average F1-Score (AF1) which is the average of all class F1-scores. The F1-score for a class $\mathcal{C}$ is defined as the harmonic mean of its precision $p(\mathcal{C})$ and recall $r(\mathcal{C})$ using the following formulas:

$$p(\mathcal{C}) = \frac{TP(\mathcal{C})}{TP(\mathcal{C}) + FP(\mathcal{C})}$$

$$r(\mathcal{C}) = \frac{TP(\mathcal{C})}{TP(\mathcal{C}) + FN(\mathcal{C})}$$

$$F1(\mathcal{C}) = \frac{2\, p(\mathcal{C})\, r(\mathcal{C})}{p(\mathcal{C}) + r(\mathcal{C})}$$

where:

- $TP(\mathcal{C})$ is the number of True Positive relatively to $\mathcal{C}$ (examples from $\mathcal{C}$ correctly classified in $\mathcal{C}$)

- $FP(\mathcal{C})$ is the number of False Positive relatively to $\mathcal{C}$ (examples not from $\mathcal{C}$ incorrectly classified in $\mathcal{C}$)

- $FN(\mathcal{C})$ is the number of False Negative relatively to $\mathcal{C}$ (examples from $\mathcal{C}$ incorrectly classified in classes other than $\mathcal{C}$)

For a problem with $N \in \mathcal{N}^*$ classes $\{\mathcal{C}_1, \mathcal{C}_2, ..., \mathcal{C}_N\}$, the AF1 can therefore be defined as:

$$AF1 = \frac{1}{N} \sum_{k=1}^{N} F1(\mathcal{C}_k)$$

All DNN models were trained using an *ADADELTA* optimiser [71] with initial learning rate $\lambda \in \{1, 0.1, 0.001\}$, 100 epochs and a batch size of 1000. The results of both classification approaches in both setups are summarised in Table 1.3.

AF1 (%)	Subject-dependent	Subject-independent
HCF [53]	91.49	28.85
MLP	32.60	26.74
CNN	34.95	15.99
LSTM	35.27	27.83

Table 1.3: Average F1-scores for the classification of happiness, frustration, boredom and other. For the subject-dependent case, the AF1 averaged over all 5 folds is reported.

Two main phenomena can be observed from those results:

- The difficulty for both HCF or DNN to obtain satisfying results in the subject-dependent case. Both classification approaches perform relatively similarly, with an AF1 only marginally better than the average guess for a 4-class problem. A possible explanation of such underwhelming performances are the difficulties mentioned in Section 1.2.2 related to the high-intraclass variability of emotion recognition problems. It can also be noted that such a phenomenon is exacerbated by the train/test split chosen: the testing set containing multiple different subjects makes obtaining good classification performances more difficult than if a leave-one-subject-out cross-validation were used, for instance.

- The large gap in performances between HCF and DNN in the subject-dependent case. The good performances of HCF show that it is possible to obtain a classifier suitable for real life use in this configuration. The tested DNN solutions however yield significantly worse performances compared to HCF. It is hypothesised that the small sample size of the *ELISE* dataset did not allow DNN models with a sufficient complexity to be trained. An analysis of the confusion matrices revealed that DNN models struggled to obtain proper recognition performances for the least represented classes of the dataset (frustration in particular). Using data rebalancing techniques (e.g. dominant class downsampling, class weights during the training phase, etc.) did not lead to any improvements.

Based on such results, it was decided to use a subject-dependent emotion classifier for the first *ELISE* prototype. To obtain satisfying emotion classification results on "unseen" test subjects, a *calibration phase* consisting of acquiring emotion-related data and labels before the actual serious game in VR was proposed. The data of the calibration phase was then used to train a personalised classifier to maximise the quality of the player experience.

Conclusion and outlook

Emotion recognition is a difficult topic regardless of whether video or physiological modalities are used, as highlighted by the example provided in this Section. Confronted with difficulties such as high intra-class variability or challenges to obtain proper emotion-related labelled data, researchers in the field have mainly focused on training subject-dependent systems, i.e. classifiers able to reliably predict the emotional states of the subjects it was trained for. The literature has shown that obtaining proper classification results was possible in this configuration even with DNNs on some specific datasets [68, 69]. The experiments carried out in the frame of the *ELISE* project confirmed that reasonable classification results could be obtained with subject-specific models. A calibration phase to acquire physiological data from the subject playing the *ELISE* serious game to train a personalised emotion recognition model was therefore proposed.

The usefulness of subject-dependent classifiers remains limited in practice, mainly because training a classification system specifically for one subject is costly in time and not very compatible with a real-time usage of such a system. Obtaining a subject-independent emotion classifier on the other hand remains a complex challenge, with only a few pieces of work attempting to tackle this [66, 67].

1.2.3 Example 2: *PainMonit* - sensor-based pain recognition

The following subsections describes a second example illustrating the difficulties of applying DNNs on time-series data in practice. Experimental results reported in this section were carried out in the frame of the research project *PainMonit* funded by the BMBF (grant number: 01DS19008A) and reported in one conference publication (ITIB 2020 [72]). The project aims to obtain a system for automatic *Pain Recognition (PR)* using physiological data as input (GSR, ECG, EMG, Heart Rate). Section 1.2.3 firstly provides an overview of the research field of PR and its challenges. Section 1.2.3 then describes the *PainMonit* project itself in more detail. Section 1.2.3 describes the dataset acquired in the frame of the *PainMonit* project. Section 1.2.3 presents experiments and results carried out in the frame of this project. Section 1.2.3 finally provides a general overview of the project and proposes future steps to be carried out in order to expand on the obtained results.

Definition and challenges

Pain is defined as "an unpleasant sensory and emotional experience" by the International Association for the Study of Pain [73]. It is often associated with situations where parts of the body are damaged, and therefore regarded as a symptom of a medical condition requiring treatment. Recognising pain properly has a high importance in the medical field as pain management is an important part of the work of the medical staff, and can influence chosen treatments.

Pain being a subjective experience, its assessment has mainly relied on verbal feedback from the patient with the help of *pain scales* until now. Pain scales can be more or less complex, ranging from simple Numerical Rating Scales (NRS) - where patients are asked to provide a number estimating their level of pain - to comprehensive questionnaires where patients are asked specific questions to characterise their health condition. Examples of such questionnaires include the McGill pain scale [74] which requires the subject to provide a score on a four-point scale to 72 different adjectives usually used to characterise pain (e.g. sharp, heavy, aching, etc.), or the Brief Pain Inventory [75] which questions to the subject about the severity of pain and its impact on some common daily functions (e.g. walking, sleeping, working, etc.).

In many situations however, the subject might not be able to communicate their level of pain (e.g. patients with cognitive disabilities, in coma, young infants, etc.). In those circumstances, the traditional approaches relying on verbal feedback or questionnaires fail. Some past works have attempted to propose pain assessment made by an external observer which would not require the intervention of the patient. An example is provided by the *COMFORT* pain scale [76] which proposes to calculate a pain score based on the observation of some physical characteristics of the patient such as facial tension, presence or absence of crying, respiratory distress, etc. Such a scale, however, does not guarantee an accurate assessment of the subject's pain level, especially if no physical manifestation can be seen.

As a result, attempts to use machine learning techniques to obtain automatic pain assessment systems using sensor data have been made over the past years. In practice, machine learning techniques summarise the PR problem either as a classification (e.g. recognition of "no pain", "low pain", "high pain", etc.) or regression problem (i.e. prediction of a value estimating the pain intensity). Despite both approaches being explored, past works have highlighted the difficulty of even an apparently simple problem such as classification of "no pain" vs "pain" [77, 78]. It can be noted that regression problems are typically more difficult than classification ones, as the model tries to predict a very specific value, unlike for classification where only a broad category is estimated. In particular, regression problems tend to require much larger amounts and much more precisely labelled data than classification ones. As a result, it is not surprising that most past works have been using a classification framework instead of a regression one. In particular, the standard classification problem consists of a binary classification between "no pain" and a specific pain level (e.g. low, medium or high) [79, 80, 81, 77, 78, 82].

To achieve proper recognition rates, the sensor modalities which provide data for the training of the classifier must be properly chosen. Past literature in the pain research field has focused on two types of modalities:

- *Behavioural modalities* which acquire data providing information about the behaviour and physical appearance of the subject (e.g. cameras, in particular RGB).

- *Physiological modalities* which acquire data monitoring the internal reaction of the body when confronted to pain (e.g. wearable devices recording GSR, EOG, EEG, etc.).

The term "behavioural modalities" has been used to refer to vision sensors nearly exclusively in past research. Based on the assumption that the face of a subject in pain could provide the most information regarding their state, facial RGB cameras have in particular been the main state-of-the-art approach for a long time. Traditionally, works using facial images for pain detection relied on the detection of specific facial landmarks (e.g. contours of the eyes, mouth, jawline, etc.) using either holistic, constraint-local-model-based or regression-based detection algorithms proposed in the literature [83]. Once detected, landmarks were tracked over successive frames, features were computed for each of them, and sent to a classifier outputting a pain prediction [84, 85, 86]. More recently, the progress obtained by deep learning for object detection has led researchers to forego the step of landmark detection and directly use DNNs on facial RGB images to output a pain prediction [87, 88, 89]. Outside of RGB images, some pieces of work have explored other video modalities such as depth or thermal imaging [90, 91] but their results indicate that using such modalities might not be much better than traditional RGB cameras.

Using video modalities, however, leads to problems similar to those already mentioned for emotion recognition in Section 1.2.2, such as the difficulty to properly set up cameras in real-life conditions, privacy concerns, etc. Behavioural-based systems also simply might not work in situations where the patient is unable to move, which are frequent in the medical field (e.g. coma, under anaesthesia, etc.). As a result, it has been attempted to use alternative sensor modalities. A growing interest has especially been observed for physiological data acquired by wearable sensors which are much less intrusive than cameras, leading to the emergence of the *sensor-based pain recognition* field. Several past works have shown that commonly used physiological modalities such as GSR, EMG, ECG could be successfully used for PR [92, 93, 94, 80, 81, 78]. More specifically, the vast majority of the aforementioned works highlighted the strong importance of GSR modalities for PR, as well as the difficulty to properly distinguish between "no pain" and "low levels of pain". "Satisfying" recognition performances were consistently attained for the classification of "no pain" vs "high pain", on the other hand.

In order to obtain the best possible recognition performances, several studies have also attempted to simultaneously use both behavioural and physiological modalities, and were often complemented by an analysis of the importance of each sensor modality used individually for PR [95, 77, 78, 82]. It was shown that the fusion of both modalities could indeed improve recognition performances for the binary classification of "no pain" vs any pain level, but only marginally compared to using only the best type of modalities. It was also observed that physiological modalities perform marginally to significantly better than behavioural ones, with GSR being the single most useful modality for PR. Finally, even the fusion of modalities could not significantly improve performances for the binary classification of "low pain" vs "no pain" [95, 77, 78, 82]. In the light of such findings, recent studies have started to mostly focus on sensor-based PR using physiological modalities, to the detriment of behavioural-based pain recognition.

Sensor-based PR is nowadays a very active research field due to the importance of its practical applications in the medical field. While the results currently achieved by past works look promising - in particular for the binary classification of "no pain" vs "high pain" - obtaining better recognition performances remains a difficult task due to reasons closely related to the ones described for sensor-based emotion recognition in Section 1.2.2. Firstly, the quantity of publicly available data is low because of the challenges surrounding the pain induction process to record pain-related data. Even though the question of the best method to properly induce pain in healthy individuals is still up for debate, solutions mostly based on heat-based stimulation [90, 96], electric-based stimulation [91] or both [97] have emerged. But their application requires extra care and specific equipment to induce pain without any risk of inadvertently causing damage to the subject. This - added to the necessity of preparing a data experimental setup which would fulfil ethical criteria - greatly limits the number of institutions able to acquire such data.

The second major obstacle slowing down sensor-based PR research is the difficulty of acquiring accurate pain labels which are necessary for the application of supervised learning machine learning approaches. Pain being a subjective experience creates many challenges, such as the difficulty to design an experimental protocol which would reliably induce pain for all subjects, or the difficulty to obtain reliable pain labels based on the patient's feedback (since precisely estimating one's own pain level is not an easy task). The first point is usually addressed in practice by having a calibration phase before the actual pain induction session to determine subject-specific pain thresholds and adapt the intensity of the pain stimuli accordingly. Regarding the second point however, no specific solution - outside of providing proper instructions and labelling tools (e.g. Visual Analog Scale) - has been found until now to increase the reliability of the subject's feedback.

Finally, the subjectivity of experiencing pain raises the difficulty to train a "universal" PR model which would correctly provide estimations for all subjects, in a similar way to sensor-based emotion recognition as reported in 1.2.2. Unlike emotion recognition however, past works in the pain research literature have reported decent performances in a subject-independent setup, especially for the simplest problem of binary classification of "no pain" vs "high pain" [79, 80, 81, 77, 78, 82]. Consequently, the binary classification of "no pain" vs "pain level x" (with $x \in \{low, medium, high\}$) in a subject-independent setup has de facto become the main standard approach to solve when it comes to wearable PR.

The following Sections present one example of a research project carried out in the field of sensor-based PR to illustrate the contents previously described.

PainMonit

The *PainMonit* project is a research project financed by the BMBF (grant number: 01DS19008A) which started in February 2019 and is still on-going at the time of writing of this thesis. This project is a collaboration between various German and Polish partners involving the Institute of Experimental Psychophysiology (IXP) of Düsseldorf, the Institute of Medical Informatics of the University of Lübeck led by Prof. Grzegorzek, the chair of Physiotherapy of the University of Lübeck led by Prof. Lüdtke on the German side, and the Department of Informatics and Medical Devices of the Silesian University of Technology in Zabrze led by Prof. Pietka and APA Group on the Polish side.

The aim of the project is to explore approaches to obtain a system performing automatic PR in real time by analysing the data coming from various sensors (behavioural or physiological). It was in particular decided to use the three following commercially available devices:

- *Logitech C920 Webcam* (Logitech, Switzerland) to record RGB videos of the subjects' faces.

- *Empatica E4 smartwatch* (Empatica, USA) which provides real-time readings for GSR, Skin Temperature, acceleration and BVP of the subject. The device also internally computes Heart Rate (HR) and Inter-Beats-Interval (IBI) data in real-time using the BVP records.

- *RespiBAN Professional platform* (Biosignals Plux, Portugal) which provides real-time data for GSR, EMG, ECG and respiration of the subject.

A preliminary study including only physiological modalities (whose results are reported in [72]) was carried out at the University of Lübeck. The data from both the *Empatica* wristband and *RespiBAN* device were collected in real-time using a software platform developed by APA Group, and then synchronised to a sampling frequency of $100Hz$. In total, $S = 10$ sensor channels were obtained from both devices.

Data acquisition

A small dataset of 10 healthy subjects (7 male, 3 female) recruited among the personnel and students of the University of Lübeck (Germany) was collected. It was decided to induce pain via heat in a similar way as [90]. For this, a *PATHWAY* machine with *CHEPS* thermode (Medoc, Israel) was used to inflict heat stimuli ranging from 32 to 49°C on the forearm on the non-dominant side

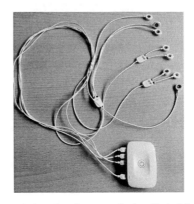

Figure 1.10: Wearable sensor devices used in the frame of the PainMonit data acquisition process: Empatica E4 smartwatch (left) and RespiBAN Professional multimodal platform (right).

of the subject. Subjects were asked to rate their pain level on a 100-point scale (0: no pain; 100: unbearable pain) using a *CoVAS* slider (Medoc, Israel) in real time.

Figure 1.11: Devices used to induce and record pain in the frame of the PainMonit data acquisition process: Medoc PATHWAY (left), Medoc CHEPS thermode (top right) and Medoc CoVAS slider (bottom right).

Because of significant differences in the pain tolerance of the individuals asked to participate in the study, a calibration procedure was performed before the actual induction phase to determine subjective temperature thresholds. The method of *staircase* was used to determine the threshold *pain50* which corresponds to the temperature at which the subject reports a pain level of 50 out of 100 on the *CoVAS* scale. Successive 10-second heat stimuli were inflicted to the subject with increments of 1°C, starting from a baseline non-painful temperature of 32°C and never exceeding 49°C. The calibration phase ended as soon as the temperature corresponding to *pain50* was reached. Depending on the value of *pain50*, a stimulation interval of temperatures $[T_1, T_2]$ of fixed length equal to six (i.e. $T_2 - T_1 = 6$) was defined for the induction phase following Table 1.4.

pain50 $\in$	T_1	T_2
$[32, 43[$	40	45
$[43, 44[$	41	46
$[44, 45[$	42	47
$[45, 46[$	43	48
$[46, 49]$	44	49

Table 1.4: Values of the heat stimulation interval $[T_1, T_2]$ depending on *pain50*. All values are given in degree Celsius.

Once the stimulation interval determined, the *Empatica* and *RespiBAN* devices were placed on the subject following the procedure described in [72]: the *Empatica* smartwatch was placed on the subject's non-dominant arm while the various RespiBAN electrodes were placed on the subject's upper body part as shown in Figure 1.12. 48 10-second stimuli were then inflicted to the subject in a random order with 8 stimuli per temperature of the induction interval. Resting phases of a length taken at random between 20 and 30 seconds were inserted between two consecutive heat stimuli. During the inter-stimuli period, the temperature of the *CHEPS* thermode was set to a non-painful temperature of 32°C. The subjects were instructed to rate their pain level continuously using the *CoVAS* slider during the whole pain induction phase. The temperatures of the thermode for the induction phase were also recorded to provide additional labelling information.

Experiments and results

A pain classifier was trained on the dataset described in the previous section using a standard supervised learning approach. While stimuli temperatures have mostly been used in the literature to label heat-induced pain data [90], it was decided to test the *CoVAS* labels as well in the frame of this study. The experiments described in this section were therefore carried out twice, once using temperature and the other with the *CoVAS* ratings.

The data records obtained from the 10 subjects were segmented in 10-second data frames either centred on pain stimuli to provide pain-related examples or extracted from the inter-stimuli intervals to provide examples of "no pain". To extract "painful" data frames, a simple peak detection algorithm based on value comparison of neighbouring samples was applied on the label records (i.e. either

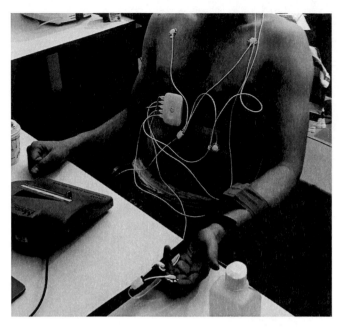

Figure 1.12: Example of sensor setup for pain data acquisition in the frame of the PainMonit project. The CHEPS thermode and Empatica smartwatch are placed on the subject's non-dominant arm (right). The RespiBAN is placed on the subject's chest, and its electrodes recording various physiological signals on the subject's upper body part (center). During the pain induction, the subject rates their pain level using a CoVAS slider (left).

temperature or *CoVAS*) to detect the onset and offset of each peak. The 10-second data frame was then centred on the middle point between the onset and offset of the peak. Details on the total number of frames extracted this way are summarised in Table 1.5.

Label type	# *pain* frames	# *no pain* frames	Total # frames
CoVAS	350	1060	1410
Temperature	460	905	1365

Table 1.5: Number of frames obtained after segmentation on the data from the 15 subjects of the *PainMonit* dataset.

Because of the fairly small size of the dataset, it was decided to translate the PR problem into a binary classification of "no pain" vs "pain" instead of "no pain" vs "pain level x" more commonly used in the literature. Separating data frames corresponding to low pain and high pain would have led to a number of "low" or "high pain" examples in single-digits for some subjects. This decision was further motivated by the fact that a subject-independent evaluation setup

44

with a leave-one-subject-out cross-validation was selected, to draw an approximate comparison with previous works of the literature also using this setup. The evaluation of the performances of the trained classifiers on less than 10 examples for a class was not deemed to be reliable enough. It can be noted that the binary classification of "no pain" against "pain" has a difficulty level in-between "no pain" vs "low pain" and "no pain" vs "high pain". Past works in the literature using behavioural, physiological or both modalities have shown that if good results could be obtained for "no pain" vs "high pain" (around 80 to 90% accuracy reported in most papers [79, 80, 81, 77, 78, 82]), results only slightly better than a random guess was the norm for "no pain" vs "low pain" [79, 80, 81, 77, 78, 82]. For the classification problem adopted in the *PainMonit* study, intermediate results were expected as the presence of "low pain" examples - which have been shown to be hardly distinguishable from "no pain" - offsets the "high pain" examples for which good classification performances are expected. All extracted data frames were therefore annotated for those two classes. For temperature labels, a "pain" label was attributed if the induced temperature was higher than the non-painful baseline of 32°C and "no pain" otherwise. For *CoVAS* ratings, data frames were labelled as "pain" as long as they were associated with *CoVAS* values strictly higher than zero, and otherwise annotated as "no pain".

Similarly to what was described in Section 1.2.2, two approaches were tested to train the pain classifier:

- **HCF:** the traditional approach consisting of manually computing features on each sensor channel of a data frame, which has remained the main state-of-the-art approach for sensor-based PR until now. The list of extracted features is provided in Table 1.6 and includes features computed on both time and frequency domains taken from various past works of the literature [79, 98, 78]. In total, 141 features were computed on a single data frame. The 141-dimensional feature vectors were then used to train a Random Forest (RF) classifier whose number of trees was fine-tuned by grid search.

- **DNN:** several types of DNNs were tested including MLPs, CNNs, residual CNNs [99] and LSTM networks. Standard normalisation was applied on each channel of the data frames of the training set before sending them as input of the networks. Training normalisation constants were then re-used to normalise the frames of the testing set. The hyper-parameters of each DNN model were fine-tuned by trial and error. Only the performances of the best model - residual CNN [99] - are reported in the following subsections.

Performances of both approaches were evaluated using the Accuracy (Acc) which is defined as

$$Acc = \frac{TP + TN}{TP + TN + FP + FN}$$

in a binary classification problem, and the Average F1-score (AF1) already defined in Section 1.2.2. The results of both approaches for both types of labels are

Sensor modality	Source	Features
EDA & EMG	[79]	max, amplitude (max-min), standard-deviation (std), inter-quartile range, Root Mean Square (RMS), mean value of local maxima, mean absolute value (mav), mav of the 1st differences, mav of the 2nd differences on raw and standardised signals
ECG	[98]	mean of RR-intervals, RMS of successive RR differences, mean of std of RR-intervals, slope of the linear regression of the RR-intervals in their time-series
HR & IBI	None	mean, std, max, min
BVP & Respiration	[78]	mean, mav and std of the 1st and 2nd order derivatives computed on both raw and standardised signals; max peak, amplitude, mean values of maxima and minima skewness and kurtosis computed on the raw signal; mean, std, area, median and spectral entropy computed on the power spectrum of the signal

Table 1.6: Hand-crafted features computed on each sensor channel of each data frame of the *PainMonit* dataset

provided in Table 1.7 and confusion matrices in Table 1.8.

Label type	Temperature		*CoVAS*	
	Acc (%)	AF1 (%)	Acc (%)	AF1 (%)
HCF	**66.91**	52.73	**75.57**	56.01
DNN	58.54	**56.27**	66.49	**59.10**

Table 1.7: Classification performances of "no pain" vs "pain" for both HCF and DNN approaches using the temperature and *CoVAS* labels of the *PainMonit* dataset. The reported evaluation metrics are averaged over all folds of the leave-one-subject-out cross validation. The best performance between HCF and DNN is highlighted in bold for both types of labels.

The main observations taken from Tables 1.7 and 1.8 are as follows:

- Both DNN and HCF approaches obtain relatively similar performances in terms of Acc and AF1 for both temperature and *CoVAS* labels. HCF yield better accuracies while DNN obtain slightly better AF1.

- The confusion matrices however reveal that both DNN and HCF approaches behave differently with HCF having a high rate of false negatives (i.e. "pain" examples classified as "no pain"), while DNN yields true positve and negative rates closer to the random guess level.

	Approach	Class	Estimated labels			
			CoVAS		Temperature	
			No pain	Pain	No pain	Pain
True labels	HCF	No pain	**90.85**	9.15	**89.72**	10.28
		Pain	77.14	**22.86**	78.70	**21.30**
	DNN	No pain	70.19	29.81	59.89	40.11
		Pain	43.71	**56.29**	43.26	**56.74**

Table 1.8: Confusion matrices of "no pain" vs "pain" for both HCF and DNN approaches using the temperature and *CoVAS* labels of the *PainMonit* dataset. All values are given in %.

- Despite not being directly comparable to the results previously reported in the literature, the classification performances for "no pain" vs "pain" fall in-between those of "no pain" vs "low pain" and "no pain" vs "high pain" as expected.

- Better classification performances are obtained using *CoVAS* labels instead of temperature ones, suggesting that subjective feedback on pain might be better to label the data.

While displaying some promising results for the classification problem of "no pain" against "pain", the study presented in this Section did not led to clear conclusions on the efficiency of one classification approach over the other due to the limited amount of data acquired so far. Further data acquisition sessions involving a higher number of participants and more painful heat-stimuli are expected to happen in the coming years of the *PainMonit* project. Classifiers for the recognition of pain excluding "low pain" stimuli will be trained to compare their performances to those obtained in past sensor-based PR works.

Conclusion and outlook

While carried out in an arguably small scale, the *PainMonit* preliminary study presented in the previous Sections illustrated well some general trends also widely observed in the literature until now. The first one is the difficulty to obtain proper classification performances with physiological modalities when "low pain" examples are involved [79, 80, 81, 77, 78, 82]. The second is the mediocre performances of deep learning compared to traditional hand-crafted feature approaches for sensor-based PR. On the one hand, DNNs have proven their strength at learning powerful features in several application domains, including behavioural-based PR as shown by the increasing number of publications recommending the use of such models on facial RGB images [87, 88, 89]. On the other hand, the number of past works reporting better DNN results than HCF for the processing of physiological time-series data obtained by wearable devices remains surprisingly low [100, 101] and limited in scope (e.g. small self-acquired datasets, single sensor modality for [101]). It can also be noted that among those papers, some give hand-crafted features as input of their models instead of raw data [80, 98], therefore using DNNs as classifiers rather than feature learners.

The reasons explaining this phenomenon are not completely clear for now. It could be argued that the quantity of available pain labelled data might not be sufficient to train the complex deep learning architectures required to learn the necessary features. The number of public benchmark datasets for PR remains fairly low, with the most notable example being the *BioVid heat-pain dataset* [90] which aggregates behavioural and physiological data with a heat-based pain induction protocol similar as the one used in *PainMonit*, and on which the vast majority of pain studies have been carried out so far. The constitution of an alternative pain dataset containing both behavioural and physiological modalities, as well as both objective (temperature) and subjective pain labels (CoVAS) is therefore an important objective of the *PainMonit* project.

1.3   Thesis contributions

The present thesis attempts to address the questions mentioned in Section 1.2.1 by summarising the findings in the main conference [52, 53, 72], and journal publications [10, 102] of the author of the thesis. The scientific contributions of this work can be split into the following main categories:

Feature extraction for time-series classification: The topic of feature extraction in time-series data is investigated in the frame of various applications of ubiquitous computing. Various time-series feature extraction methods ranging from traditional feature engineering to popular feature learning approaches based on deep learning are tested for three applications using time-series classification: sensor-based Human Activity Recognition (HAR), emotion recognition and pain recognition. Comparative frameworks allowing a fair comparison of feature extraction approaches are defined and used in experiments to highlight their respective performances, and determine which one is the best suited for each application. Results indicate that deep feature learning does not necessarily always outperform traditional feature extraction methods. State-of-the-art classification performances are also obtained on various datasets related to all three tested applications by their respective best performing approach.

Deep feature learning for HAR: The relevance of deep feature learning for time-series classification is analysed more specifically in the frame of one of the most popular application fields of ubiquitous computing: sensor-based HAR. HAR is characterised by a relative simplicity of the data and label collection process compared to other application fields of ubiquitous computing, due to movement-based sensors such as accelerometers, gyroscopes or Inertial Measurement Units (IMUs) being widespread, and a relatively low intra-class variability (i.e. different individuals will perform the overall same movement to accomplish a gesture despite some differences in executions). As a result, a relatively large amount of data has been collected for HAR-based applications over the past years [103, 104], leading to a large number of studies from the machine learning community. While many of them have highlighted the potential of deep learning for time-series classification in a HAR context [9, 8], none had taken the initiative to properly compare it to other traditional machine learning approaches in a fair comparison framework. In Li et al. [10] published in the journal *Sensors* (MDPI), a comprehensive review and comparative analysis of various state-of-the-art time-series feature extraction approaches is carried out on two benchmarks of sensor-based HAR: the OPPORTUNITY [103] and UniMIB-SHAR [104] datasets. The study in particular proposes to test various popular deep-learning-based feature learning techniques, including both supervised and unsupervised ones. The results of those studies reported in this thesis highlight the superiority of supervised deep learning approaches compared to other traditional feature extraction methods for time-series classification in HAR.

Deep transfer learning using time-series: A new transfer learning method - introduced in a journal article published in *Sensors* (MDPI) [102] - is proposed in this thesis to enhance the performances of DNNs for time-series classification in a context of limited data availability. It was designed to be employed without requiring assumptions on the similarity between the source and target domains, and to be usable for multi-channel time-series data, thus addressing the main limitations of current approaches from the literature. Inspired by past transfer-learning-related achievements reported in the image processing literature [46], it proposes to build a source dataset containing heterogeneous time-series data coming from diverse sensor modalities obtained from various datasets proposed in the literature. A source task consisting of the supervised classification of sensor modalities is defined on the source domain. The internal parameters of a DNN trained for such a source task and accepting single-channel inputs are then transferred to a multi-channel DNN architecture trained to solve the target problem on the target dataset. This method is tested for two completely different applications of ubiquitous computing: sensor-based HAR and emotion recognition. The results of the study reported in this thesis show that such a transfer strategy allows the target DNN to yield better performances than in the case where transfer learning was not used on both application domains.

1.4 Overview

This thesis is structured into two main Chapters, each describing works carried out by the author of this thesis to address both questions evoked in Section 1.2.1.

Chapter 2 describes the works carried out to address the first question raised in this thesis about the benefits of using deep learning compared to other traditional machine learning methods for time-series classification, and more specifically the comparative analysis carried out for sensor-based HAR reported in [10]. An overview of HAR and the traditional machine learning pipeline used to achieve it is firstly performed. It is followed by a comprehensive review of related works attempted in the literature to build HAR systems. The works carried out in the frame of the comparative study are then described, starting with a description of the comparative framework and the state-of-the-art time-series classification approaches. The experiments, their results and their analysis are finally examined.

Chapter 3 describes works carried out to address the second question raised about the practical application of deep learning for time-series classification, and more specifically the new time-series transfer learning approach based on sensor modality discrimination on the source domain reported in [102]. A theoretical description of transfer learning in both machine and deep learning contexts is firstly performed, followed by an analysis of related works found in the literature. The methodology of the transfer learning method is then described in detail, before presenting the experiments, their results and related analysis.

Finally, Chapter 4 performs a summary of the findings reported in the frame of this thesis, in particular to which extent they addressed both questions raised in Section 1.2.1 regarding the application of deep learning for time-series classification. It ends with an analysis of the work required to improve and extend the proposed approaches and a discussion of future works.

Chapter 2

Deep learning for sensor-based human activity recognition

2.1 Problem statement

In this Section, the reasons for the investigation of deep learning performances in the field of wearable Human Activity Recognition (HAR) are laid out. A description of the basic pattern recognition concepts required for such investigation is also provided. Parts of the contents of this Section are strongly inspired by the *Sensors* (MDPI) publication Li et al. [10].

2.1.1 Motivation

The two examples provided in Section 1 are illustrative of the potential difficulties of applying deep learning for ubiquitous computing applications using time-series data. In both examples, DNNs led to the learning of relatively poor features compared to traditional machine learning approaches relying on manual feature crafting based on expert knowledge. While DNNs could yield performances relatively comparable to hand-crafted features for wearable-based pain recognition (*PainMonit* study presented in Section 1.2.3), they were clearly outperformed in the context of wearable-based emotion recognition (*ELISE* study presented in Section 1.2.2). The exact reasons for such underwhelming performances remain to be investigated, but are hypothesised to be caused by two main factors:

- **Low amounts of data**: collecting labelled data is a complex process which is expensive in terms of both time and resources for any application related to ubiquitous computing. In both examples provided in Section 1, this issue is exacerbated by the complexity of placing the subjects in a state where the desired kind of data would be obtained - although for different reasons. On the one hand, finding methods to reliably induce specific emotions is a research topic still relatively unexplored. The proposed emotion induction protocols used in the frame of the *ELISE* study were observed to be effective on most tested subjects, but at the same time did not have the expected effect on others, leading to less data than expected being acquired for some emotional classes. On the other hand, data acquisition in *PainMonit* was made more difficult by the sensitive nature of pain induction from an ethical point of view. Such considerations for instance led to a limitation on the number or intensity of pain stimuli inflicted to the subjects, hence resulting in lower amounts of collected data.

- **High intra-class variability**: both emotions and pain have the particularity to be highly subjective experiences. This can lead to very high *intra-class variability* - i.e. large differences in data of the same class but taken from two distinct subjects - which makes the task of finding class boundaries which would remain relevant for all individuals much more difficult. To make matters even more complicated, high intra-class variability can also be observed in the data collected from a single subject. Phenomena of pain sensitisation (i.e. increased sensibility to pain) and habituation (i.e. increased tolerance to pain) are for instance well documented in the literature [105] and can lead an individual to rate their pain levels differently when confronted to the same pain stimuli.

In order to check the potential benefits of DNNs for time-series classification compared to traditional machine learning models, it is therefore preferable to carry out studies in an application domain less affected by the two aforementioned factors. The most natural candidate for such an analysis is the field of wearable HAR. Over the past years, HAR has established itself as the most popular field of study of ubiquitous computing for several reasons. Wearable HAR firstly relies on user-friendly and affordable movement sensors such as accelerometers and gyroscopes. Movement data is also usually relatively easy to annotate which simplifies the process of obtaining the labels required to apply supervised learning approaches. Finally, HAR is less affected by issues related to intra-class variability than other ubiquitous computing applications. Past HAR works have proposed to draw a distinction between *atomic activities* which refer to very basic short movements, and more complex activities - usually composed of a sequence of atomic activities - referred to as *composite activities* [106, 107]. While the execution of composite activities might greatly vary when performed by different subjects, the simplicity of atomic activities usually leads to a strong reduction in such inter-subject differences, and as a consequences in intra-class variability.

The aforementioned factors have led to a strong interest from the ubiquitous computing research community towards HAR. Many researchers have proposed their own set of atomic activities to study [108, 103, 104, 109, 102], leading to a quantity of available annotated data notably larger than for other ubiquitous computing applications. This favourable context for machine learning studies has consequently led to a high number of studies being carried out to evaluate the performances of diverse algorithms for activity recognition, including DNNs which have yielded promising performances so far. But the high variety in datasets, proposed sets of activities, data partition strategies, and sometimes the lack of provided implementation details have made a direct comparison of such different algorithms difficult. In this context, it remains in particular difficult to assess how deep-learning-based approaches really perform compared to more traditional machine learning approaches, and whether it is really worth going through the complex process of training DNNs instead of using simpler approaches.

Those observations highlight the strong need for a study comparing different machine learning approaches for wearable HAR in a fair and standardised framework. Such study was carried out and published in the *Sensors* journal (MDPI) in Li et al. [102], and is described in details in this Section. The following Subsections provide a more in-depth description of HAR, and describe the fundamental concepts of machine learning used in the comparative study.

2.1.2 Human activity recognition

Human Activity Recognition (HAR) is a topic which, in the wake of the development and spread of increasingly powerful and affordable mobile devices or wearable sensors, has attracted an increasing amount of attention from the research community. The main goal of HAR is automatic detection and recognition of activities from the analysis of data acquired by sensors. HAR finds potential applications in numerous areas, ranging from surveillance tasks for security, to assistive living and improvement of the quality of life or gaming [110, 107].

To provide a suitable framework for the application of machine learning techniques, HAR is usually abstracted as a classification problem. Each activity to recognise corresponds to one class. A classification model - also referred to as *classifier* - is trained to provide scores estimating how likely its input data are to belong to each class. The class with the highest score is then selected as the system prediction. Machine learning approaches train a classifier based on the analysis of annotated data to provide a system which would correctly predict the class of each input data as often as possible.

While the aforementioned principles can be applied with any data, large differences in machine learning approaches can be observed in practice based on the type of data used for HAR. A distinction is in particular made in the literature between two main types of modalities:

- **Video-based HAR** which refers to HAR achieved using video data which captures information about the movements of the subjects [111]. Video-based HAR is achieved by placing camera sensors - usually RGB - in the environment surrounding the subjects to monitor.

- **Sensor-based HAR** (sometimes also referred to as wearable HAR) which refers to HAR achieved using time-series data coming from movement sensors placed on the body of the subject to monitor [107, 112]. The most commonly used sensors for sensor-based HAR are Inertial Measurement Units (IMUs) which provide mainly acceleration and angular velocity information.

While both video and sensor-based HAR are still active research topics nowadays, a strong growing interest in sensor-based HAR has been observed over the past decade. This trend can be explained by several reasons. On the one hand, cameras are confronted with several difficulties which hinder their practical use. Their usefulness is for instance very dependent on their setup which must allow them to capture videos from the same specific viewpoint used to train the HAR models. Their recognition performances tend to be strongly affected by possible perturbations in the background or variations in human appearance due to clothing [111]. Additionally, the acquisition of video data on which individuals can easily be identified can be the source of data privacy concerns. On the other hand, motion sensors such as IMUs have seen their affordability and practicability drastically increase over the past years in parallel of the expansion of ubiquitous computing. The ever increasing pervasiveness of mobile devices containing IMUs in everyone's daily life such as smartphones or smartwatches has also lowered the difficulty of acquiring data to train HAR classifiers, and re-using trained models in real conditions [107]. The studies described in [10] and reported more in detail in this Chapter were carried out in a sensor-based HAR context due to the aforementioned reasons. The contents of the following Subsections will therefore mainly focus on sensor-based HAR from this point on.

2.1.3 Pattern recognition chain

The development of an HAR system typically follows a standardised sequence of actions involving the use of sensor engineering, data analysis and machine learning techniques. Figure 2.1 illustrates this process -referred to as *Activity Recognition Chain (ARC)* [113]- which comprises five ordered steps: data acquisition, data pre-processing, segmentation, feature extraction and classification. A detailed description of each step is provided in the following Subsections.

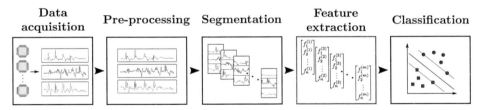

Figure 2.1: The Activity Recognition Chain (ARC).

Data acquisition

The data acquisition step encompasses all operations required to obtain the data and their associated labels (if supervised learning approaches are used) needed to train machine learning models. Those include in particular:

- **Choice of activities to recognise (i.e. classes):** such choice is mostly dependent on the context in which the trained model is expected to be used. It can be noted that this process is not standardised in the literature. The vast majority of past works on sensor-based HAR define their own sets of activities to recognise. While some works proposed to make a distinction between atomic (i.e. short and basic) and composite (i.e. long and complex) activities [106, 107], no agreement has been found on a common set of atomic (nor composite) activities and this point remains an open research question.

- **Choice and setup of wearable sensors:** such choice is usually impacted by the nature of activities to be recognised, or potential issues such as obtrusiveness, energy consumption, difficulty to setup on the subject, etc. [107]). IMUs are the most commonly encountered devices in sensor-based HAR studies, due to their cheapness, easiness to use and ability to provide useful movement information (acceleration and angular velocity). The location of the sensors is another important factor to take into account since the same sensor device but placed on different body parts will usually return significantly different data.

- **Choice of the dataset size:** the question of how much data should be acquired to properly train a classifier with machine learning is usually difficult to answer and has remained an open research question until now. On the one hand, acquiring a large quantity of diverse data is important to obtain a recognition model able to generalise well outside of the training set and avoid overfitting. On the other hand, the process of data collection and labelling is quite expensive in terms of time, resources and subjects in practice. As a result, most studies usually opt for a compromise between those two opposing principles by picking as many subjects as possibly allowed by resources available to them.

- **Choice of the labelling strategy:** labels are annotations which indicate to which activity the recorded data can be associated with, and usually chosen as integers in $\{1, 2, ..., C\}$ with $C \in \mathcal{N}^*$ total number of classes. Attributing labels to the data is a very important part of any project relying on supervised machine learning, and choosing how to do it can affect the experimental design. In the sensor-based HAR literature, two main labelling strategies have been used. The first - referred to as *timestamp-based labelling* - consists of continuously annotating the data over time to provide one annotation at each time a data point was obtained. This process is usually performed by asking experts to carefully analyse and note down specific timestamps at which activities start or end in videos of the subjects contributing to the data acquisition process (e.g. [103]). While it allows to provide the most accurate annotations, this labelling strategy is also extremely costly in terms of setup complexity (e.g. preparation of additional cameras recording the whole scene), time and manpower to provide the annotations. For this reason, simpler strategies such as *event-based labelling* which consists of attributing one single annotation to a whole data record containing a single or several repetitions of the same activity have also been used [104, 109, 102].

It can be noted that the data acquisition step is always one of the most important steps of the ARC in HAR studies. This is due to several reasons. Firstly, machine learning approaches depend on large quantities of data to ensure a proper training of recognition models. Additionally, numerous choices made at that stage can impact the difficulty of the classification problem to solve such as the nature of the activities which were chosen to be recognised, or the number and placement of sensors used to acquire the data.

Data pre-processing

Data pre-processing refers to all operations required to improve data quality and make them suitable for further analysis. Some of the most widely used pre-processing techniques for HAR include:

- **Denoising**: an imperfect setup of sensors, hardware failure, or external factors related to the environment in which the data were acquired are all possible reasons which can lead to noisy data. Denoising aims at fixing this issue by using post-data-collection operations on the acquired time-series signals. The most common examples of denoising operations are filtering approaches which aim at leaving out parts of the original signals which would not contain useful information for further processing, either by analysis of the frequency components of the signals using Fourier transform, or by convolution of the signals with some specific filter.

- **Normalisation:** using multiple sensor devices to acquire data can usually produce time-series data with very different value ranges depending on which sensor channel they are coming from. Such discrepancies can cause some channels to become preponderant compared to others in further steps of the ARC. To address this, normalisation techniques can be applied to align all data channels on a common value scale. The most widely used examples of normalisation approaches are standard normalisation which translate and rescale the original signals to yield new ones of zero mean and unit variance, and min-max normalisation which projects data values into the $[0, 1]$ range.

- **Channel synchronisation:** another issue sometimes appearing in multi-modal setups is discrepancies in the data format obtained by difference sensor devices. The different sampling frequencies of the various devices lead to time-series data records of different lengths which can complicate further processing operations. To address this issue, downsampling or upsampling the data channels which would have a higher or lower sampling frequency than the target synchronisation frequency can be performed by using data interpolation techniques.

It can be noted that the choice of the data processing operations to be used for a specific application is completely dependent on the dataset acquired to train the models, i.e. some datasets might require the application of a large number of data-processing techniques while others might not require any. All operations should also be applied on the whole dataset and not specific subsets (e.g. data from specific subjects) in order not to introduce any bias and properly train the HAR system.

Segmentation

The pre-processed data acquired after the two first phases of the ARC can contain significant amounts of data if the latter were recorded over long periods of time. In those conditions, it may be necessary to apply a segmentation approach to cut the original data records into smaller segments containing relevant information about the activities to be recognised. This step serves two main purposes. On the one hand, it filters the data by excluding parts irrelevant to the recognition problem. On the other hand, it reduces the quantity of data to be processed by the subsequent stages of the ARC by extracting segments of limited size. This last point especially matters in practice, as hardware-related constraints can limit the amount of data which are possible to process at each time step.

The *sliding-window approach* is one of the simplest and most widely used segmentation methods for time-series records. A window size corresponding to a fixed duration (e.g. one second) is firstly chosen, usually by taking into account characteristics of the activities to recognise such as their average duration. The window is then slid on the original data records to produce data segments of the chosen temporal length. For the processing of multimodal time-series data, segments are usually 2D matrices of shape $T \times S$ where $T, S \in \mathcal{N}^*$ designate respectively the number of sequential data points during the chosen time length and the number of sensor channels. This process can be performed with or without overlapping between successive segments.

More elaborate segmentation methods can also be used for sensor-based HAR. The two main alternative strategies include *energy-based segmentation* which extracts data segments in portions of the original data records where some monitored value ("energy") exceeds some pre-defined threshold (e.g. around times where the magnitude of the acceleration is high) [113, 104], and *contextual segmentation* which uses information provided by additional sensor modalities (e.g. GPS, audio signals, etc.) to find times in the original records where extracting a data segment would be meaningful [113].

For all the aforementioned approaches, a label indicating its associated class (i.e. activity in the case of HAR) is attributed to each data segment. The labelling strategy of segments is dependent on how the original data signals were annotated. For event-based labelling, segments can be labelled with the annotation given to the event corresponding to the data records they were extracted from. For timestamp-based annotation, the most common labelling strategy consists of attributing the majority label of all timestamps contained in the segment to the whole data segment.

Feature extraction

Feature extraction designates the computation of *features* from the segmented data, i.e. specific values which could carry high relevance to the considered classification problem. Feature extraction is one of the most important steps of any supervised machine learning problem and achieves three main goals. The first is to provide an abstracted representation of the data which is easier to use than the data segments to train the mathematical classification models. Some parameters such as the sampling frequency of the devices used to acquire data or the chosen segmentation window length can lead data segments to contain a large number of values, which could significantly increase the complexity of the classification model using them as inputs. The second is the removal of information in the data which would not be relevant to the considered classification problem such as noise still remaining after the pre-processing operations, or data acquired before and after an activity for HAR. Allowing the classifier to consider only useful information during its training has shown to significantly increase the simplicity of the training process and improve the final classification performances. Finally, the third reason to extract features before training classifiers is to avoid overfitting. Choosing features providing a high-level representation of the data segments is important to make sure the models are not learning the training data and their details too well, thus increasing the chances that the trained models will generalise on unseen data.

Features can be computed from the data in different ways. Two main strategies for feature extraction can generally be considered:

- **Feature engineering:** the most traditional approach which consists of computing a set of features chosen based on intuition or expert knowledge about the data and classification problem at hand [114, 107, 112].

- **Feature learning:** approaches which attempt to obtain features in an automated way by letting models analyse the data to find the most relevant features by themselves. The popularity of feature learning has notably increased over the past years with the rise of deep learning [32].

Once extracted from a data segment, features are concatenated to yield a *feature vector* $\mathbf{x} \in \mathcal{R}^F$ where $F \in \mathcal{N}^*$ is the dimensionality of the feature space. It can be noted that F can be greater than the actual number of features if some features computed on the data segments are multidimensional. Each segment and its corresponding label is then associated with one feature vector, yielding a labelled dataset used to train the classification model. In the following sections, a labelled dataset of $N \in \mathcal{N}^*$ examples $\mathbf{x}$ will be referred to as $(\mathcal{X}, \mathcal{Y})$ where $\mathcal{X} \in (\mathcal{R}^F)^N$ designates the dataset and $\mathcal{Y} \in \{1, 2, ..., C\}^N$ designates the labels associated to each element of $\mathcal{X}$.

Classification

The classification step refers to the process of training a classification model - also referred to as *classifier* - on the acquired labelled dataset $(\mathcal{X}, \mathcal{Y})$. Classifiers attempt to find a boundary to separate the examples $\mathbf{x} \in \mathcal{X}$ of two or more classes in the feature space $\mathcal{R}^F$. For most classifiers, the determination of the optimal boundary is performed by firstly defining a *loss function* $\mathcal{L}_\theta$ - dependent on the parameters of the classifier θ - which returns a value estimating how close the model predictions were to the expected outputs. An optimisation algorithm is then applied to find the optimal model parameters θ which minimise $\mathcal{L}_\theta$ on the dataset $(\mathcal{X}, \mathcal{Y})$.

The training algorithm used to minimise the loss on a given dataset is highly dependent on the type of classification model used. Extensive mathematical theoretical works have been carried out in the past to provide nowadays standardised and commonly used classifiers. The most popular examples include Support-Vector-Machines (SVM) [34], Random Forests (RF) [115], probabilistic classifiers relying on Bayes theory [116] or Softmax classification [19].

Training a classifier on a given dataset is a task whose difficulty increases with the complexity of the dataset and given classification problem due to the so-called *bias-variance trade-off* [117]. The trained classifier is usually required to be able to generalise on subjects who did not provide data for the training set to be useful for practical applications. This objective must be achieved while trying to minimise two different sources of error: the *bias error* which increases when the classifier underfits its training data, i.e. learns wrong assumptions from the data when finding the decision boundary, and the *variance error* which is caused by overfitting, i.e. the model learning too well some specificities of the dataset. Having large quantities of available data for the training process can help minimise both errors.

The training of a classifier is always performed following a standardised procedure which consists of separating the dataset $(\mathcal{X}, \mathcal{Y})$ into two distinct subsets called respectively the *training set* $(\mathcal{X}_{train}, \mathcal{Y}_{train})$ and the *testing set* $(\mathcal{X}_{test}, \mathcal{Y}_{test})$. The data contained in the training set are used to train the classifier, i.e. fed to the training algorithm to update the classifier parameters during the loss optimisation. The data of the testing set are used to evaluate the performances of the trained classifier, i.e. fed to the trained model to provide estimated labels $\tilde{\mathcal{Y}}_{test}$) whose proximity to the true labels $\mathcal{Y}_{test}$) is evaluated using evaluation metrics. In some studies, an additional set - distinct from both training and testing sets - called the *validation set* $(\mathcal{X}_{val}, \mathcal{Y}_{val})$ is also used to specifically fine-tune the parameters of the model during the training process: classifiers with different sets of parameters are trained as usual on the training set and their performances are evaluated and compared on the validation set. The model with the highest validation performance is finally selected and evaluated on the testing set.

It can be noted that having strictly distinct training and testing (and validation if applicable) sets is key in avoiding a large variance error. The most basic solution consists of choosing arbitrary thresholds to split the set $(\mathcal{X}, \mathcal{Y})$, e.g. 80%/20% of the data for the training and testing sets respectively (or 70%/10%/20% for training, validation and testing). More elaborate approaches can also be considered to further increase chances of the trained classifier to generalise well on unseen data. The most frequently used one is the *k-fold cross validation* strategy which involves splitting the set $(\mathcal{X}, \mathcal{Y})$ into $k \in \mathcal{N}^*$ parts of approximately same size $(\mathcal{X}_i, \mathcal{Y}_i)_{1 \leq i \leq k}$ (referred to as *folds*), using each $(\mathcal{X}_i, \mathcal{Y}_i)$ as testing set and the other subsets $(\mathcal{X}_j, \mathcal{Y}_j)_{1 \leq j \leq k, j \neq i}$ as training set for $1 \leq i \leq k$, and then averaging the evaluation metrics obtained on all folds.

2.2 Related work

The rising popularity of sensor-based HAR over the past years has led to a large and diverse literature. In this Section, an overview of the main proposed HAR approaches is given. The approaches are categorised by type of feature extraction methods, with a distinction between approaches relying on feature engineering, and those on feature learning, with a specific focus on deep learning.

2.2.1 Feature engineering

After preliminary works carried out in the late 1990s hinted at the fact that human activities could lead to changes of values in physiological signals [118], researchers attempted during the past decades to propose methods to compute features able to capture such changes as well as possible. Initially tested because of their high simplicity, simple features based on the computation of basic statistical descriptors on the time-series data showed to be quite effective in providing meaningful information for the distinction of human activities. In [119], acceleration, temperature, light and audio data acquired for six simple activities (including sitting, standing, walking, ascending/descending stairs, running) were collected by six subjects using a home-made multi-sensor platform. The study of the data showed that even very simple features exclusively computed on the time-domain of each - such as mean, standard-deviation, zero-crossing rate, percentiles, etc. - sensor channel separately could lead to high classification performances with Decision Trees (DT) and Naive Bayes (NB) classifiers. In [120], a home-made multimodal platform recording audio, movement and environmental data was used for the recognition of 21 Activities of Daily Living (ADLs) such as brushing teeth, washing face, making tea, etc. The features used for classification with Coupled Hidden Markov Models and Factorial Random Fields involved statistical metrics computed on the time domain of the acceleration and audio signals, but also correlation-based features computed between pairs of accelerometer channels, and frequency features computed on the magnitude of the Fourier Transform (FT) of the signals such as spectral entropy and spectral energy. The authors of [121], proposed to complement "statistical features" - referring to the previously mentioned simple metrics computed on either the time or frequency domain of each sensor channel - with "physical features" which consisted of specific metrics based on expert-knowledge, whose computation usually involved computations on multiple sensor channels. Their proposed features were successfully applied for the classification of nine activities (walk forward/left/right, go upstairs/downstairs, sit, jump up, stand up) using a linear SVM and data coming from an accelerometer and gyroscope placed on the right front hip of 6 subjects. In [113], a small study for the recognition of 11 ADLs involving hand movements (e.g. open/close window, drink, water plants, etc.) was carried out using three IMUs placed on the dominant arm of two subjects. Several feature configurations were tested including simple statistical features computed on the time domain of each sensor channel or frequency-based features such as spectral energy, entropy, cepstral coefficients. A comprehensive comparative study of various state-of-the-art classifiers such as k-Nearest Neighbours (kNN), SVM, NB, Hidden Markov Models (HMMs), Discriminant Analysis (DA), Joint Boosting (JB) was also carried out. The studies showed that the best classification performances could be obtained with both time and frequency features mixed together and SVM or kNN classifiers. In [122], a similar study was carried out for the recognition of 12 activities (walking, standing up, standing, sitting in various positions, etc.) with six subjects wearing a multimodal sensor platform with three IMUs worn on the chest, right thigh and left ankle of the subjects. The performances of statistical features computed on both time and frequency domains of the signals was compared to those of directly using the segmented data without feature extraction. Several classifiers including SVM, Decision Trees (DT), kNN, Gaussian Mixture Models (GMMs) were tested in a study which showed that directly using the raw data was inferior to performing feature extraction. kNN proved once again to be the best of the tested classifiers.

The consistency of simple statistical features computed on both time and frequency domains in obtaining good classification performances for HAR has led researchers to explore feature selection approaches instead of attempting to propose their own features. In [121], three different feature selection strategies including Relief-F [123] (filter), Single Feature Classification (wrapper) and Sequential Forward Selection (wrapper) were evaluated on statistical and "physical" features for the classification of nine activities. The study showed that feature selection could lead to significant improvements compared to not using any, with Sequential Forward Selection performing the best. In [124], a study comparing the performances of three filter selection approaches - Relief-F, Correlation-based Feature Selection and fast Correlation-based Filter - was performed on a set of statistical features extracted on the time domain of accelerometer and gyroscope signals coming from a smartphone placed on the subjects' right front hip. The study using data from six classes (sitting, standing, lying down, performing large/small movements, walking up/down the stairs) acquired from 44 subjects also showed significant improvements in classification performances after using any of the three tested feature selection methods. In [125], a study was carried out on a dataset of 77 subjects who performed 24 different activities (e.g. walking on a treadmill at different speed and inclination settings, driving a car, brushing teeth, etc.) while wearing a single 3D accelerometer attached to their belt. Three filter feature selection approaches - Relief-F, correlation-based and expert-based feature selection - were tested on a set of various statistical features computed on both time and frequency domains of the signals. The results of the study showed that feature selection could again improve classification performances compared to not using any, with all three tested methods yielding similar classification performances.

The aforementioned hand-crafted features have shown to yield decent recognition results for sensor-based HAR, but their simplicity has also led researchers to try to find whether more complex features could even further improve classification performances. Designing elaborate and specialised hand-crafted features is however a complex process which gives little guarantee that the obtained features would be optimal nor generalisable to other HAR applications than the one they were designed for. For this reason, a growing interest of the sensor-based HAR community in feature learning approaches has been observed over the past years. This trend has in particular coincided with the rise of popularity of deep learning approaches, which have exhibited remarkable capabilities as feature learners in other application domains, especially including images [32].

2.2.2 Deep feature learning

The rise in popularity of feature learning approaches for sensor-based HAR has coincided with the developments of deep learning based approaches over the past years, and the publication of a large variety of sensor-based HAR benchmark datasets gathering IMU data which made the training of such approaches easier, such as *OPPORTUNITY* [103] (daily life activities), PAMAP2 [126] (daily life and sport activities), Daphne Gait [127] (activities related to the monitoring of Parkinson's disease), UCF HAR [128] (basic activities such as walking, sitting, standing, etc.), Actitracker [129] (sport-related activities) or *Skoda* [108] (activities specifically related to car manufacturing). The first attempts at feature learning for sensor-based HAR focused on unsupervised deep learning approaches. In [130], a method based on Restricted Boltzmann Machines (RBMs) [131] was compared to regular statistical feature engineering and feature extraction with Principal Component Analysis (PCA) [132] on four sensor-based HAR datasets (including *OPPORTUNITY* and *Skoda*). In addition, a data pre-processing step using an Empirical Cumulative Distribution Function (ECDF) prior to feature extraction was tested. ECDF was used to provide an alternative representation of the data which would standardise input data ranges while preserving the data structure. The results showed that PCA with ECDF and RBM with or without ECDF yielded the best performances on all four tested datasets. In [133], several approaches centred around Autoencoders (AEs) [134] were tested on the UCF HAR dataset. Two feature learning - sparse AE and denoising AE - and two feature engineering approaches - statistical and PCA - were used to obtain features to train a SVM classifier. The experiments showed that sparse AEs yielded the best classification performances while the other tested feature learning methods obtained performances comparable to the feature engineering ones.

Feature learning with supervised DNNs was also attempted and displayed promising results compared to feature engineering or unsupervised feature learning. In [135], a CNN model with "partial weight sharing", i.e. convolutional kernels whose weight values depend on which part of the input they are processing (instead of being replicated on the whole input like traditional CNNs), was proposed to learn HAR features. It was compared to several other supervised and unsupervised feature learning methods including regular CNN, MLP, MLP with PCA applied on its input, RBM. The experiments carried out on the *OPPORTUNITY*, *Skoda* and *Actitracker* datasets showed the superiority of CNNs with partial weight sharing over the other tested approaches. In [136], a model based on Deep Belief Networks (DBNs) [137] was tested on the *Antitracker*, *Daphne Gait* and *Skoda* datasets. A model with fully-connected layers was firstly greedily pre-trained in an unsupervised way. A Softmax classification layer was then added to fine-tune the ensemble in a supervised way. This method yielded the best performances on the three datasets out of several approaches including MLPs and statistical features. In [138], a simple CNN architecture taking 2D data frames as input was tested on the *OPPORTUNITY* dataset and a small dataset of hand gestures. It was compared to other methods such as SVM or kNN on raw data, mean and variance of the sensor channels as features or DBN taking vectors of channel means as inputs. The proposed CNN outperformed all other approaches on both tested datasets. In [9], a hybrid architecture combining convolutional and Long-Short-Term-Memory (LSTM) cells [31] was proposed for the classification of activities on the *OPPOR-TUNITY* and *Skoda* datasets. This approach was tested against various feature engineering methods proposed in the past literature on *OPPORTUNITY*, and some deep feature learning approaches relying on simple CNNs proposed in the literature for *Skoda*. The proposed hybrid architecture outperformed all other approaches on both datasets. In [8], a comparative study focusing on deep learning models for feature engineering was carried out on the *OPPORTUNITY*, PAMAP2 and Daphne Gait datasets. Several architectures including MLP, CNN, LSTM taking frames of data as inputs, sequence-to-sequence LSTMs or bi-directional LSTMs were tested and their performances compared to each other. The study showed the superiority of convolutional and recurrent (LSTM) architectures compared to MLP which was found to be very sensitive to changes in hyper-parameters such as number of layers or units per layer. It also showed that CNN tended to perform better on datasets containing long and repetitive activities such as PAMAP2 while LSTM-based models performed better on the two other datasets containing shorter activities. In [139], a hybrid approach between feature learning and engineering was proposed and tested on a home-made dataset of 30 subjects performing six activities (standing, sitting, laying, walking, walking up/downstairs) with one smartphone attached to their waist. It consisted of training a "teacher model", i.e. a shallow MLP with simple statistical features computed on both time and frequency domains of the signals. A "student model", i.e. a deep LSTM model taking raw time-series data as input was then trained using the softmax outputs of the teacher model as labels. The decisions of both teacher and student models were then fused together by considering the argmax of the sum of their softmax outputs to provide a final class estimation. Several experiments involving the use of the teacher and student models alone or together were carried out. They showed that using raw data as input with shallow classification (e.g. MLP) performed worse than taking manually crafted features as inputs, and that deep-classification on raw data with LSTM could yield very slightly improved performances compared to shallow learning. The fusion of shallow and deep learning yielded better performances and compared favourably to regular CNN-based architectures taken from the literature.

The literature about non-deep-learning-based feature learning methods is far less comprehensive and explored. The only notable approaches fitting into this category are the *codebook approaches* (also sometimes referred to as *bag-of-words approaches* [140]) which build a feature representation of the data in an unsupervised way by finding characteristic data segments - *codewords* - after application of a clustering algorithm. The occurrence frequencies of the learned codewords are then used as features to represent the original data records. Examples of the application of such approaches in sensor-based HAR include [141] which demonstrated the superiority of codebook approaches over statistical feature engineering on a home-made dataset of smartphone accelerometer data acquired by three subjects carrying out commuting activities (still, walking, travelling by train/tram/metro/bus). Similarly, [142] highlighted the superiority of codebook approaches compared to various feature engineering methods taken from the literature on one EOG dataset of cognitive activities (e.g. copying a text, reading a paper, taking handwritten notes, etc.) and one accelerometer dataset of simple physical activities (e.g. jumping in place, clapping hands, waving, etc.).

It should be noted that all the aforementioned studies - both regarding feature engineering and feature learning - were carried out in a large variety of evaluation frameworks. Despite some benchmark datasets being frequently used in the past literature (especially *OPPORTUNITY*), each study used its own set of data and activities, its own classifier and evaluation metrics, and its own set of baseline models to perform performance comparisons with its proposed approach. Additionally, two studies using the same datasets might not use the data in the same way, e.g. the training of the classification models might be performed in a subject-dependent way in some configurations, while a subject-independent data split might be adopted in another one. All those aforementioned factors make a direct comparison of all approaches proposed in the past literature quite difficult. Evaluating the respective performances of feature engineering against feature learning, or of different feature learning approaches against each other is especially complicated. Those reasons highlight the need of a fair comparison study carried out in a standardised evaluation framework.

2.3 Comparative study of feature learning approaches

2.3.1 Comparative framework

Experience has shown the final recognition performances of an HAR system to be very dependent on every step of the ARC. While many extensive theoretical studies have also been carried out in the past decades to establish powerful - and nowadays standardised - classification models such as SVM or softmax classification, most of the focus has been put recently on the feature extraction stage, as the effectiveness of the classification is directly impacted by the quality of the obtained feature representation. Feature engineering has traditionally been the most common approach for a long amount of time. However, such an approach is not always possible in practice, for instance when the structure of the input data is unknown a priori because of a lack of expert knowledge in the domain. Additionally, there is no guarantee for features crafted manually to be optimal. For this reason, finding more systematic ways to get good features has drawn an increasing research interest [33].

Notable progress has been done recently to find feature learning techniques allowing models to automatically learn features from data with minimal or even no manual input. Solutions using DNNs have especially exploded in popularity in the past few years. Past works in the literature have highlighted the ability of DNNs to learn strong discriminative features, with each feature being encoded by one of their neurons [32]. DNNs can in particular craft highly abstract features by stacking hidden layers, which enables the computation of high-level features on the low-level descriptors encoded by the first layers of the network. The ways to re-use learned features are also increased by the higher number of possible connections between input and output neurons [33]. As a consequence, deep learning based models have exhibited strong performances in classification problems using either image [143] or time-series modalities [33], in particular in a sensor-based HAR context [8, 9].

However, despite the promising results obtained, it in fact remains difficult to rigorously assess the efficiency of feature learning methods, especially deep learning related ones. As highlighted in Section 2.2, direct comparisons between the performances of different approaches can be challenging because of a lack of standardisation regarding the ARC steps: differences in the benchmark HAR dataset(s), data pre-processing operations, segmentation techniques and parameters, or classification models are all obstacles hindering this goal. To tackle this issue, an evaluation framework where all stages of the ARC *except the feature extraction step* are fixed (as shown in Figure 2.1) is proposed in Li et al. [10], taking inspiration from the comparative study carried out for image classification in [144]. This framework enables an evaluation and comparison of different feature learning models on a fair and objective basis. Specifically, it is used to perform comparative studies on two public benchmark datasets: *OPPORTUNITY* [103] and UniMiB-SHAR [104].

2.3.2 Feature learning approaches

This section succinctly presents the feature learning approaches selected in our comparative study. Seven different feature extraction approaches were tested, covering most of the recent state-of-the-art ones in HAR described in Section 2.2, for both feature engineering or learning:

- **Hand-crafted Features (HCF):** involving the computation of simple statistical metrics on the data: this approach constitutes a baseline in our comparative study as the only feature engineering method.

- **Multi-Layer-Perceptron (MLP):** the most basic type of ANN featuring fully-connected layers. The MLP approach provides baseline results for supervised feature learning using ANNs.

- **Convolutional Neural Network (CNN):** a class of ANN featuring convolutional layers which contain neurons performing convolution products on small patches of the input map of the layer, thus extracting features carrying information about local patterns

- **Long Short-Term Memory network (LSTM):** one of the most popular variant of Recurrent Neural Networks which feature layers containing LSTM cells, able to store information over time in an internal memory.

- **Hybrid model featuring CNN and LSTM layers:** taking advantage of the high modularity of ANN-based architectures, previous studies in sensor-based HAR reported that hybrid architectures can extract features carrying information about short and long-term time dependencies, and yield better performances than pure CNNs or LSTM networks [8, 9].

- **Autoencoder (AE):** a class of ANNs trained in a fully unsupervised way to learn a condensed representation which leads to the most accurate reproduction of its input data on its output layer. The results obtained by this approach are used as a baseline for unsupervised feature learning.

- **Codebook approach (CB):** an unsupervised feature learning method based on the determination of "representative" subsequences - referred to as *codewords* - of the signals used for the learning. The ensemble of codewords - referred to as *codebook* - is then used to extract histogram-based features based on similarities between subsequences of the processed data and codewords.

The following subsections will present each of the seven aforementioned methods in more details.

Hand-crafted features

The manual crafting of features has for a long time been the most common way to train a machine learning model for a specific classification problem. In order to maximise the likelihood of the features being useful, experts in the classification problem at hand are asked to provide suggestions on which features would be relevant to monitor. Hand-crafted features can take many different forms and have various levels of computation complexity since they are strongly dependent on the type of acquired data and classification problem to solve.

Manually crafting features based on expert knowledge has shown to yield satisfying results in practice. But asking the opinion of an expert is not always possible, either because of a lack of resources and time, or just the lack of expertise in the specific target problem. In those conditions, a commonly used solution when time-series data are involved consists of computing a large number of low-level features on the signals such as mean, standard-deviation or other simple statistical metrics, either on the time or frequency domain [113]. Such features are computed individually on each sensor channel of the data segments in cases where multiple modalities are involved, and then concatenated to form a feature vector. Despite its simplicity, this approach has shown to yield fairly good results in practice for sensor-based HAR [120, 121, 113, 122].

It can be noted that computing a large amount of simple statistical metrics on the data can lead to using suboptimal features, or features even detrimental to the classification problem. For this reason, a *feature selection* approach is sometimes additionally applied to determine the features of a given set which would be the most beneficial. Two main families of feature selection methods were identified in [145] and [146]:

- **Filter methods:** these approaches attempt to filter out irrelevant features independently of the classification method employed, i.e. before the training of a classifier, usually by establishing a feature ranking on the basis of specific metrics. The most notable examples of filter methods include Mutual Information and Correlation Criteria [146].

- **Wrapper methods:** these approaches are based on proposing a strategy for selecting specific subsets of the original feature set, training the classifier with the selected features, and evaluating its classification performances. The performances obtained for each tested subset are then compared to determine the optimal set of features. Prominent examples of wrapper methods include Recursive Feature Elimination, Sequential Selection algorithms and Heuristic Searches [146].

Both filter and wrapper feature selection approaches have their advantages. Wrapper methods tend to select a subset of features closer to the optimal one than filter methods due to the large number of combinations of features they test. They are however also quite expensive to apply both in terms of time and computational resources, making them impractical in configurations where the size of the original feature set is large.

Codebook approach

Codebook approaches are methods inspired by bag-of-word feature extraction methods proposed in the image processing literature [147] and which have been successfully re-applied in a context of time-series classification [148] and sensor-based HAR [142].

The idea behind the codebook approach is based on two consecutive steps, illustrated in Figure 2.2. The first step - codebook construction - aims at building a codebook by applying a clustering algorithm on a set of subsequences extracted from the original data sequences. Each center of the clusters obtained this way is then considered as a *codeword* which represents a statistically distinctive subsequence. The second step - codeword assignment - consists of building a feature vector associated to a data sequence: subsequences are firstly extracted from the sequence, and each of them is assigned to the most similar codeword. Using this information, a histogram-based feature representing the distribution of codewords is then built.

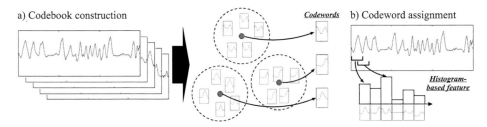

Figure 2.2: An overview of the codebook approach.

For the codebook construction step, a sliding time window approach with window size $w \in \mathcal{N}^*$ and sliding stride $l \in \mathcal{N}^*$ is firstly applied on each sequence to obtain subsequences (w-dimensional vector). A k-means clustering algorithm [149] is then employed to obtain $N \in \mathcal{N}^*$ clusters of similar subsequences, with the Euclidean distance used as similarity metric between two subsequences. It can be noted that the outcome of k-means clustering can be dependent on the initialization of the cluster centers, which is performed at random. The clustering algorithm was therefore run ten times, and the result for which the sum of the Euclidean distances between subsequences and their assigned cluster centres is minimal were selected. At the end of this step, a codebook consisting of N codewords is obtained.

For the codebook assignment step, subsequences are firstly extracted from a sequence using the same sliding window approach employed in the codebook construction step. For each subsequence, the most similar codeword is determined. A histogram of the frequencies of all codewords is then built, with the bin corresponding to one codeword being incremented by one each time the codeword was considered as the most similar to one of the subsequences. The histogram is finally normalised so that the sum of the N codeword frequencies yields one to obtain a probabilistic feature representation.

68

The approach described above is referred to as "codebook with *hard assignment*" (from now on abbreviated as CBH) since each subsequence is deterministically assigned to one codeword. This approach however might lack flexibility to handle "uncertain" situations where a subsequence is similar to two or more codewords. To address this issue, a *soft assignment* variant (referred to as CBS) is therefore proposed to perform a smooth assignment of a subsequence to multiple codewords based on kernel density estimation [150].

Assuming that $\mathbf{x}_s$ and $\mathbf{c}_n$ are the sth subsequence ($1 \leq s \leq S$) in a sequence and the nth codeword ($1 \leq n \leq N$), respectively, the smoothed frequency $F(\mathbf{c}_n)$ of $\mathbf{c}_n$ is computed as follows:

$$F(\mathbf{c}_n) = \frac{1}{S} \sum_{s=1}^{S} \frac{K_\sigma(D(\mathbf{x}_s, \mathbf{c}_n))}{\sum_{n'=1}^{N} K_\sigma(D(\mathbf{x}_s, \mathbf{c}_{n'}))}, \qquad (2.1)$$

where $D(\mathbf{x}_s, \mathbf{c}_n)$ is the Euclidian distance between $\mathbf{x}_s$ and $\mathbf{c}_n$, and $K_\sigma(D(\mathbf{x}_s, \mathbf{c}_n))$ is its Gaussian kernel value with the smoothing parameter $\sigma \in \mathcal{R}^{+*}$. The closer $\mathbf{x}_s$ is to $\mathbf{c}_n$ (i.e., the smaller $D(\mathbf{x}_s, \mathbf{c}_n)$ is), the larger $K_\sigma(D(\mathbf{x}_s, \mathbf{c}_n))$ becomes, or, in other words, the bigger the contribution of $\mathbf{x}_s$ to $F(\mathbf{c}_n)$ becomes. In this way, soft assignment allows to obtain a feature which represents a smoothed distribution of codewords taking into account the similarity between all of them and the subsequences.

Multi-layer perceptron

Multi-Layer Perceptron (MLP) is the simplest type of ANN and involves a hierarchical organisation of neurons in layers. MLPs comprise at least three fully-connected layers (also called *dense layers*) including an input, one or more intermediate (hidden) layers and an output layer, as shown in Figure 2.3. Each neuron of a fully-connected layer takes the outputs of all neurons of the previous layer as its inputs. Considering that the output values of hidden neurons represent a set of features extracted from the input of the layer they belong to, stacking layers can be seen as extracting features of an increasingly higher level of abstraction, with the neurons of the nth layer outputting features computed using the ones from the $(n-1)^{th}$ layer.

Convolutional neural networks

Convolutional Neural Networks (CNNs) belong to a class of ANNs which comprise convolutional layers featuring convolutional neurons. The kth layer is composed of n_k neurons, each of which computes a convolutional map by sliding a convolutional kernel $(f_T^{(k)}, f_S^{(k)})$ over the input of the layer (indicated in red in Figure 2.4). Convolutional layers are usually used in combination with activation layers, as well as pooling layers. The neurons of the latter apply a pooling function (e.g.,

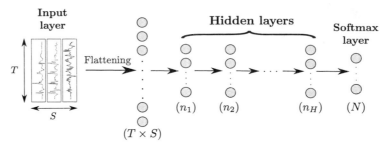

Figure 2.3: Architecture of a MLP model with H hidden layers for sensor-based HAR. Input data from the different sensor channels are first flattened into a $(T \times S)$-dimensional vector and then fed to the hidden layers. All layers are fully-connected. The numbers in parenthesis indicate the number of neurons per layer. T, S and N designate the time length of the input data, the number of sensor channels, and the number of classes, respectively.

maximum, average, etc.) operating on a patch of size $(p_T^{(k)}, p_S^{(k)})$ of the input map to downsample it (indicated in blue in Figure 2.4), to make the features outputted by neurons more robust to variations in temporal positions of the input data. Convolution and pooling operations can either be performed on each sensor channel independently ($f_S^{(k)} = 1$ and/or $p_S^{(k)} = 1$) or across all sensor channels ($f_S^{(k)} = S$ and/or $p_S^{(k)} = S$).

Similarly to regular dense layers, convolutional-activation-pooling blocks can be stacked to craft high-level convolutional features. Neurons of stacked convolutional layers operate a convolutional product across all the convolutional maps of the previous layer. For classification purposes, a fully-connected layer after the last block can be added to perform a fusion of the information extracted from all sensor channels. The class probabilities are outputted by a softmax layer appended to the end of the network.

Recurrent neural networks and long-short-term-memory

Recurrent Neural Networks (RNNs) are a class of ANNs featuring directed cycles among the connections between neurons. This architecture makes the output of the neurons dependant on the state of the network at the previous timestamps, allowing them to memorise the information extracted from the past data. This specific behaviour enables RNNs to find patterns with long-term dependencies.

In practice, RNNs are very affected by the problem of *vanishing or exploding gradient*, which occurs when derivatives of the error function with respect to the network weights become either very large or close to zero during the training phase [28]. In both cases, the weight update by the back-propagation algorithm is adversely affected. To address this issue, a variant of the standard neuron called Long-Short-Term-Memory (LSTM) cell was proposed [31]. The latter is designed to remember

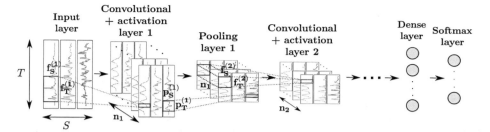

Figure 2.4: Architecture of a CNN model for sensor-based HAR. T, S and n_k designate the time length of the input data, the number of sensor channels, and the number of convolutional kernels of the kth layer, respectively. The convolutional and pooling kernels of the kth layer process patches of the input data of sizes $(f_T^{(k)}, f_S^{(k)})$ and $(p_T^{(k)}, p_S^{(k)})$, respectively. Neurons of intermediate convolutional layers perform convolution products across all convolutional maps of the previous layer.

information over time by storing it in an internal memory, and update, output or erase this internal state depending on their input and the state at the previous time step. This mechanism, depicted in Figure 2.5, is achieved by introducing several internal computational units called *gates*, each featuring their own weights, bias, and activation functions. An input, output and forget gates are used to respectively block the input of the cell (preserving its memory m_t), block its output (preventing it from intervening in the computation of m_{t+1}), and erase its internal memory at time t. All gates operate on the input vectors $\mathbf{x}_t$ of the cell at time t, and the outputs of the cell at the previous time step $\mathbf{c}_{t-1}$, following the equations

$$\mathbf{y}_t^i = \sigma_i(\mathbf{W}_i\mathbf{x}_t + \mathbf{U}_i\mathbf{c}_{t-1} + \mathbf{b}_i) \tag{2.2}$$

$$\mathbf{y}_t^f = \sigma_f(\mathbf{W}_f\mathbf{x}_t + \mathbf{U}_f\mathbf{c}_{t-1} + \mathbf{b}_f) \tag{2.3}$$

$$\mathbf{y}_t^o = \sigma_o(\mathbf{W}_o\mathbf{x}_t + \mathbf{U}_o\mathbf{c}_{t-1} + \mathbf{b}_o) \tag{2.4}$$

$$\mathbf{m}_t = \mathbf{y}_t^i \otimes \sigma_1(\mathbf{W}\mathbf{x}_t + \mathbf{U}\mathbf{c}_{t-1} + \mathbf{b}) + \mathbf{y}_t^f \otimes \mathbf{m}_{t-1} \tag{2.5}$$

$$\mathbf{c}_t = \mathbf{y}_t^o \otimes \sigma_2(\mathbf{m}_t) \tag{2.6}$$

with $\mathbf{y}_t^*$ representing the output of gate $*$ at time t for $* \in \{i, o, f\}$ (referring to input, output and forget respectively), and $\mathbf{m}_t$ indicating the memory state of the cell at time t. σ_* designates the activation function, $\mathbf{W}_*$, $\mathbf{U}_*$ the matrices of weights, and $\mathbf{b}_*$ the vector of biases of the gate $* \in \{i, o, f\}$. $\mathbf{W}$, $\mathbf{U}$ and $\mathbf{b}$ are matrices of weights and a bias vector for the input of the cell, respectively. σ_1 and σ_2 are activation functions designed to squash the input and output of the cell, respectively. $\otimes$ represents the element-wise multiplication of two vectors.

Similarly to regular neurons, LSTM cells are organised in layers, with the output of each cell being fed to its successive cell within the layer and to the next layer of the network. LSTM layers can be organized following several patterns, including in particular *many-to-many* (the outputs of all cells of the layer are used as inputs of the next one) and *many-to-one* (only the output of the last cell is used as input of the next layer). The output of the last layer can be passed to a dense and softmax layer for the classification problem.

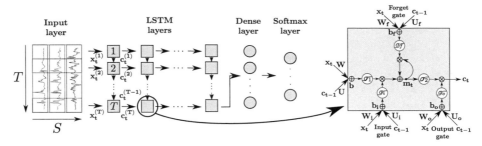

Figure 2.5: Architecture of a LSTM network for sensor-based HAR (left). The intermediate and last LSTM layers are organised in a many-to-many and many-to-one layout, respectively. Each LSTM layer is composed of LSTM cells (right). $\mathbf{x}_t$, $\mathbf{m}_t$ and $\mathbf{c}_t$ represent the cell input, memory, and output at time t, respectively. In addition, $\oplus$ and $\otimes$ refer to the element-wise addition and multiplication, respectively. $\mathbf{W}_*$, $\mathbf{U}_*$, $\mathbf{b}_*$ and σ_* designate internal weight matrices, bias vector and activation function (for gate $* \in \{i, o, f\}$). σ_1 and σ_2 are internal activation functions applied on the input and memory of the cell, respectively.

Hybrid convolutional and recurrent networks

Thanks to the high modularity of ANN architectures, it is also possible to append LSTM layers to convolutional blocks as depicted in Figure 2.6. The last convolutional block of the network produces n-dimensional time series with n being the number of neurons of the convolutional layer. This output is then sliced along the time dimension. Each slice, indicated in blue in Figure 2.6, is flattened and fed as input of a LSTM cell. The number of LSTM cells, equal to the number of slices, is dependent on the sizes of the input data, convolutional and pooling kernels of the convolutional blocks.

Autoencoder

Autoencoders (AEs) [134] are ANNs specifically designed to learn a condensed representation of the input data in an unsupervised way. This is achieved by using a specific architecture consisting of the concatenation of an *encoder* and a *decoder*, as shown in Figure 2.7. The encoder is a regular network that projects input data in a feature space of lower dimension, while the decoder - whose structure is usually the symmetric of the encoder one - maps the encoded features back to the input space. The AE is then trained to reproduce input data on its output based on a loss function like Mean Squared Errors.

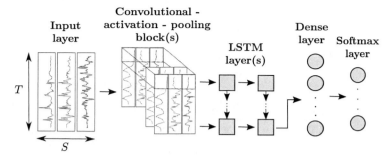

Figure 2.6: Architecture of a hybrid CNN+LSTM model for sensor-based HAR. Each slice along the time dimension of the output of the convolutional block(s) (in blue) is fed to one LSTM cell. All LSTM layers are organised in a many-to-many pattern, except the last which follows a many-to-one scheme.

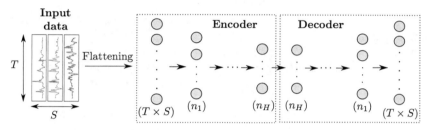

Figure 2.7: Architecture of an autoencoder model for sensor-based HAR. The numbers in parenthesis refer to the number of neurons per layer. H denotes the number of hidden layers in both the encoder and decoder.

2.3.3 Datasets

OPPORTUNITY

The *OPPORTUNITY* dataset [103] is built from four subjects performing 17 different Activities of Daily Life (ADLs), as listed in Table 2.1. A NULL class that is not related to any of the 17 ADLs is also present, bringing it to a total of 18 distinct classes. The data were collected in a controlled environment simulating a studio flat. They were acquired at a sampling frequency of 30Hz using 7 wireless body-worn inertial measurement units, providing 3D acceleration, rate of turn, magnetic field and orientation information, as well as 12 additional 3D accelerometers placed on the subjects' arms, back, hips and feet, and accounting for a total of 145 different sensor channels. Each subject was asked to perform 6 runs during the acquisition process: 5 runs - named "ADL1" to "ADL5" - following a scripted scenario leading to the subject performing all of the different activities, and a 6th specific run - named "Drill" - consisting of 20 repetitions of each of the 17 ADLs of the dataset. The data are labelled on a timestamp level, i.e. one label is associated to every sampling time.

As it can be seen in Table 2.1, the *OPPORTUNITY* dataset features a notable imbalance in favour of the NULL class which represents 72.28% of the whole

Class	Proportion	Class	Proportion
NULL	72.28 %	Open Drawer 1	1.09 %
Open Door 1	1.87 %	Close Drawer 1	0.87 %
Open Door 2	1.26 %	Open Drawer 2	1.64 %
Close Door 1	6.15 %	Close Drawer 2	1.69 %
Close Door 2	1.54 %	Open Drawer 3	0.94 %
Open Fridge	1.60 %	Close Drawer 3	2.04 %
Close Fridge	0.79 %	Clean Table	1.23 %
Open Dishwasher	1.85 %	Drink from Cup	1.07 %
Close Dishwasher	1.32 %	Toggle Switch	0.78 %

Table 2.1: Classes of the *OPPORTUNITY* dataset and their respective proportions of the dataset.

dataset. This fact is important for the evaluation phase, as the recognition rate of the dominant class might skew the performance statistics to the detriment of the least represented classes. For this reason, it is advisable to use an evaluation metric independent of the class distribution. In this study, the average F1-score (defined in Section 1.2.2) is used as main evaluation metric. In a binary classification context, the F1-score is the harmonic mean of precision (number of true positives divided by the total number of examples evaluated as positive) and recall (number of true positives divided by the number of positive elements). For a multiclass problem, the F1-score is firstly computed for each class in a one-vs-all way, and then averaged over all classes to yield the average F1-score. To make the comparison with past works easier, two additional evaluation metrics used in previous works [103, 104] were also added: the overall accuracy (number of examples correctly classified divided by the total number of examples), and the weighted F1-score (sum of class F1-scores, weighted by the class proportion).

The *OPPORTUNITY* dataset contains a certain number of sensors for which small to very large chunks of data are missing due to data transmission problems of the wireless sensors during the acquisition process. To bypass this problem, the sensor channels the most affected by this issue were removed for the purpose of this study. In total, 38 channels were removed, including data from the left and right hand accelerometers, and quaternion information from the inertial measurement units. For the remaining 107 sensor channels, the missing values were completed with the last non-missing one.

For the segmentation phase, a common sliding time-window approach consisting of extracting "frames" of data by sliding a fixed-length window was adopted. By denoting the length of the time window by $T \in \mathcal{N}^{+*}$ and the sliding stride by $\sigma \in \mathcal{N}^{+*}$, each of the obtained data segments consisted of a $T \times S$ matrix, with S (= 107) being the number of sensor channels. A time window of 2 seconds (i.e. $T = 64$) and a sliding stride of $\sigma = 3$ were adopted, following a pre-processing setup similar to the one used in [138].

It was decided to use the data from runs ADL1, ADL2, ADL3 and Drill (of all 4 subjects) for the training set, and from the runs ADL4 and ADL5 for the testing set. This led to 211,265 and 78,029 segments for the training and testing sets, respectively. All data segments were labelled using a majority labelling strategy on the timestamp level labels.

UniMIB-SHAR

The UniMiB-SHAR dataset (University of Milano Bicocca Smartphone-based HAR) [104] aggregates data from 30 subjects (6 male and 24 female) acquired using the 3D accelerometer of a Samsung Galaxy Nexus I9250 smartphone ($S = 3$). The data are sampled at a frequency of 50 Hz, and split in 17 different classes, comprising 8 ADLs and 7 "falling" actions as shown in Table 2.2. Each activity is either performed 2 or 6 times, with half of them having the subject place the smartphone in their left pocket, and the other half in their right pocket. Unlike *OPPORTUNITY*, the dataset does not feature any NULL class and remains fairly balanced, despite three ADLs classes having a sensibly higher representation (walking, running and going down).

Class	Proportion	Class	Proportion
Standing Up from Sitting	1.30 %	Falling Forward	4.49 %
Standing Up from Laying	1.83 %	Falling Left	4.54 %
Walking	14.77 %	Falling Right	4.34 %
Running	16.86 %	Falling Backward	4.47 %
Going Up	7.82 %	Falling Backward Sitting-chair	3.69 %
Jumping	6.34 %	Falling with Protection Strategies	4.11 %
Going Down	11.25 %	Falling and Hitting Obstacle	5.62 %
Lying Down from Standing	2.51 %	Syncope	4.36 %
Sitting Down	1.70 %		

Table 2.2: Classes of the UniMiB-SHAR dataset and their respective proportions. ADLs and falls are provided in the left and right column, respectively.

For this dataset, time windows of data and their associated labels are directly provided with a fixed length $T = 151$ corresponding to approximately 3 seconds. An energy-based segmentation technique was used by locating time windows centred around peaks of acceleration data [104]. A peak of acceleration is detected at time t when the magnitude of the signal is higher than $1.5g$ (with g being the gravitational acceleration constant) and lower than 0 at time t-1. The dataset contains 11,771 time windows of size 151×3 in total.

2.4 Experimental results on *OPPORTUNITY*

2.4.1 Implementation details

This Section provides more in depth details regarding the implementation of all feature extraction methods presented in Section 2.3.2. All DNN-based methods were implemented and trained on an Intel i7-7700K CPU machine with 16GB RAM and a NVidia GTX 1080Ti GPU. Codebook approaches were trained and executed on a high-performance computation server with dual Intel Xeon X5690 CPUs and 96GB RAM.

Hand-crafted features

A total of 18 hand-crafted features (15 statistical and three frequency-related; listed in Table 2.3) were used, all computed on each sensor channel of the data frames independently, following the suggestions of [112]. They were then concatenated to yield a feature vector of size $18 \times S$. To remove the effect of the discrepancies between the values taken by each feature, a min-max normalisation was performed on each feature to project its values in the interval $[0, 1]$. The normalisation constants computed on the training set were re-used for the computation of features on the testing set.

Hand-crafted features		
Maximum	Percentile 50	First-order mean
Minimum	Percentile 80	Norm of the first-order mean
Average	Interquartile	Second-order mean
Standard-deviation	Skewness	Norm of the second-order mean
Zero-crossing	Kurtosis	Spectral energy
Percentile 20	Auto-correlation	Spectral entropy

Table 2.3: List of the hand-crafted features used in our study. Each feature is computed on each sensor channel independently.

Codebook approach

Given a data segment, CB was used to extract a feature from each of $S = 107$ sensor channels. The segment was then represented using "early fusion" which simply concatenates features from all the channels into a single high-dimensional feature [142]. In this framework, a codebook for each channel was constructed using the same set of three hyper-parameters, subsequence length w, sliding stride for sampling subsequences l and number of codewords N. Since past studies have shown that a denser sampling of subsequences yields a better performance [151, 142], l was set to 1. It was also decided to use $N = 128$ based on preliminary experiments using $\{64, 128\}$ which showed that higher performances could be achieved by more detailed analysis with a larger number of codewords (larger values for N turned out to be impractical because of issues related to RAM consumption). Finally, w was set to 24 by examining $\{8, 16, 24, 32\}$. For the soft assignment approach (CBS), the codeword distribution smoothing parameter σ was set to 2^8 ($= 256$) based on prior tests with $\{2^{-5}, 2^{-4}, \cdots, 2^9\}$. In the end, each segment was associated to a $13,696$-dimensional vector ($S \times N = 107 \times 128$).

Multi-layer perceptron

A MLP was defined with three hidden layers with REctified Linear Units (RELU) activations, taking vectors obtained by flattening multimodal segments of data as inputs. It was noticed that the addition of a batch normalisation layer [152] significantly improved the classification results. Batch normalisation layers standardise the inputs of the subsequent layers by computing parameters on batches of training data to normalise each sensor channel independently. It aims to reduce the risk of *internal covariate shift*, which refers to the changes in the distributions of the inputs of a layer during the training phase, and can cause the input values to move toward the saturation regime of the activation function. This phenomenon can potentially decrease gradient values and slow down the training phase. The best performances were obtained by placing a single batch normalisation layer directly after the input of the network, although [152] recommends to place them before every activation of hidden layers. This indicates that internal covariate shift could be avoided as long as input data were normalised by a batch normalisation layer. The final architecture used for the MLP models used in the study thus consists of a batch normalisation layer, followed by three fully-connected layers with RELU activations, and an output layer with a softmax activation providing estimations of probabilities for each class. All hyper-parameters of the model and their values are summarised in Table 2.4.

Convolutional neural network

The tested CNN architecture involved three consecutive blocks, each including a convolutional, RELU activation and max-pooling layers. Each convolutional kernel performed a 1D convolution over the time dimension for each sensor channel independently. Cross-channel convolutions were not performed since preliminary experiments showed that models with such convolution kernels could degrade performances on the *OPPORTUNITY* dataset. Similarly to MLP, adding a batch normalisation layer right after the input layer yielded significant performance improvements. The model selected in the end comprised in order: a batch normalization layer, three blocks of convolutional-RELU-pooling layers, a fully-connected layer and a softmax layer. The hyper-parameters of those layers are provided in Table 2.4.

Long-short-term memory

Based on the results of preliminary experiments it was decided to use a model with two layers. The number of LSTM cells in both layers is equal to the size of the time window T. All cells of the network used the sigmoid function for the gate activations, and hyperbolic tangent for the other activations. Each LSTM cell of the first layer took as inputs the data from all sensor channels at its corresponding time, and the output of the LSTM cell processing the data at the previous time. The first LSTM layer was organised in a many-to-many manner, while the second LSTM layer followed a many-to-one outline. A batch normalisation layer was also added at the beginning, and a dense and softmax layers at the end of the network. The values of all hyper-parameters of the model are provided in Table 2.4.

Hybrid CNN and LSTM models

Using an architecture similar to the ones in [9], a network stacking batch normalisation, convolutional-RELU-pooling, LSTM, one fully-connected and one softmax layers was designed. After preliminary tests showed that increasing the number of layers did not necessarily improve the performances, it was decided to use one convolutional-RELU-pooling block and two LSTM layers on the *OPPORTUNITY* dataset. The LSTM layers were organised in the same way as the one of the LSTM model described in Section 2.4.1, with the number of LSTM cells being equal to the "time length" of the output of the convolutional-RELU-pooling block. The last LSTM layer followed a many-to-one pattern, and its output was fed to a dense layer, followed by a softmax layer. The values for the convolutional and LSTM hyper-parameters are provided in Table 2.4.

Autoencoder

A simple autoencoder model was used, with the encoder and the decoder both featuring only one dense layer. This decision stemmed from preliminary observations that increasing the number of hidden layers did not improve the classification performances, and that using layers with many neurons instead (as shown in Table 2.4) yielded a significant performance improvement. All neurons were given a RELU activation.

2.4.2 Comparative study results

The accuracies, weighted and average F1-scores of all tested feature learning approaches on the *OPPORTUNITY* dataset are summarised in Table 2.5. Supervised deep-learning-based feature extraction methods outperform other approaches by a sensible margin. The best performing method is the hybrid CNN and LSTM model (Hybrid), with a weighted F1-score of 70.86% on the *OPPORTUNITY* dataset. Although a strict comparison is not possible (because of differences in the evaluation

Table 2.4: Hyper-parameters of the deep-learning-based models found for $T = 64$ on the *OPPORTUNITY* dataset. The parameter values are given assuming that the input of the models is of size $T \times S$. Convolutional kernels and pooling sizes are, respectively, given as $(f_T^{(k)}, f_S^{(k)})$ and $(p_T^{(k)}, p_S^{(k)})$ (based on their definition in Section 2.3.2).

Model	Parameter	Value
MLP	· # neurons in dense layers 1,2 and 3	2000
CNN	· Conv. kernel size for blocks 1, 2 and 3	(11,1), (10,1), (6,1)
	· Conv. siding stride for blocks 1, 2 and 3	(1,1), (1,1), (1,1)
	· # conv. kernels in blocks 1, 2 and 3	50, 40, 30
	· Pool. sizes for blocks 1, 2 and 3	(2,1), (3,1), (1,1)
	· # neurons in dense layer	1000
LSTM	· # LSTM cells in layers 1 and 2	64, 64
	· Output dim. of LSTM cells in layers 1 and 2	600, 600
	· # neurons in dense layer	512
Hybrid	· Conv. kernel size	(11,1)
	· Conv. sliding stride	(1,1)
	· # conv. kernels	50
	· Pool. size	(2,1)
	· # LSTM cells in layers 1 and 2	27, 27
	· Output dim. of LSTM cells in layers 1 and 2	600, 600
	· # neurons in dense layer	512
AE	· # neurons in encoder & decoder dense layer	5000

frameworks which were employed), an analogy to the results obtained by several previous works such as [138, 9, 8] suggests that the obtained results are state-of-the-art.

While hybrid CNN-LSTM models performed better than using CNN or LSTM separately, it is interesting to note the sensible difference of 4.45% between the average F1-scores of LSTM and CNN. CNN (as well as CBH and CBS) can extract features containing information about short-term time dependencies in the data, with a time horizon constrained by the length of the time window T and the size of the convolutional kernels. On the other hand, LSTM can take into account long-term time dependencies thanks to the memory mechanism of LSTM cells. The observations of the obtained results seem to indicate that features detecting patterns in the long term are more important for the classification of activities on this dataset. Appending a LSTM network to a convolutional block allows the computation of features taking both short- and long-term dependencies into account.

Table 2.5: Classification performance metrics (in percent) of different feature extraction models on the *OPPORTUNITY* dataset.

Method	Accuracy	Weighted F1-Score	Average F1-Score
HC	89.96	89.53	63.76
CBH	89.66	88.99	62.27
CBS	90.22	89.88	67.50
MLP	91.11	90.86	68.17
CNN	90.58	90.19	65.26
LSTM	91.29	91.16	69.71
Hybrid	**91.76**	**91.56**	**70.86**
AE	87.80	87.60	55.62

2.4.3 Impact of input sensor channel variation

The previous experiments were carried out in a setup fixing some hyper-parameters related to the first stages of the ARC (depicted in Figure 2.1). This Section presents additional studies carried out with modifications to the data acquisition and segmentation phases to check their influence on recognition performances. The influence of the number of sensor channels and the size of the sliding time window at the segmentation stage were tested in particular.

Increasing the number of sensor channels S allows the amount and diversity of the input data to grow. However, in practice, it also complexifies the setup of the wearable devices. For this reason, it is important to check whether the tested feature extraction methods are robust to variations of S.

Additional experiments were carried out with different subsets of the 107 sensor channels. The creation of subsets was based on the principle of PCA. All sensor channels were firstly ranked by decreasing variance (computed on the full dataset). Different subsets of features were then formed by selecting the n sensor channels with the highest variance for $n \in \{5, 10, 20, 50, 80\}$. The size of the time window was kept at $T = 64$. The results for the average F1-scores are summarised in Table 2.6 and Figure 2.8.

As expected, increasing S leads to better performances for all different feature extraction methods as the variety and amount of data used to train the models increase. The relative performances of the tested approaches also remain unchanged for all numbers of sensor channels. Hybrid models still outperform all other approaches, which confirms the robustness of such deep learning architectures.

Number sensors	HC	CBH	CBS	MLP	CNN	LSTM	Hybrid	AE
5	5.35	5.81	6.53	14.94	14.25	16.25	**18.38**	5.57
10	10.36	13.38	13.50	24.57	22.63	23.50	**27.10**	5.75
20	20.32	28.34	28.88	39.29	38.47	41.89	**46.11**	9.17
50	56.75	56.35	58.52	62.68	57.08	62.23	**63.70**	42.67
80	62.50	61.10	64.93	65.82	63.23	67.36	**68.79**	51.21
107	63.76	62.27	67.50	68.17	65.26	69.71	**70.86**	55.62

Table 2.6: Average F1-scores (in percent) of the feature learning models for different numbers of sensor channels on the *OPPORTUNITY* dataset.

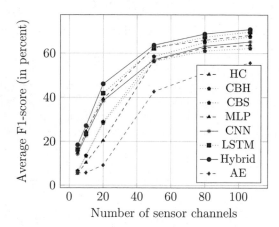

Figure 2.8: Average F1-scores of the feature learning methods on the *OPPORTU-NITY* dataset, using different numbers of sensor channels (ranked by decreasing variance).

2.4.4 Impact of segmentation parameters

The length of the sliding window T has a strong influence on the features extracted by the different feature learning models. This is especially the case for the deep learning related methods, for which a variation of the size of the input layer impacts the architecture of the subsequent layers and causes changes in the field of view of the neurons in convolutional layers, or in the number of LSTM cells of the recurrent layers.

To check whether the trends previously observed are still relevant regardless of T, two more comparative studies using $T = 32$ (approximately 1 second) and $T = 96$ (approximately 3 seconds) were carried out. The obtained results are shown in Table 2.7.

The trends observed in the reference case ($T = 64$) remained globally unchanged irrespective of the value of T. The supervised deep learning methods still achieved the best performances, with hybrid models outperforming the other methods. It

81

Method	T = 32			T = 64 (baseline)			T = 96		
	Acc.	WF1	AF1	Acc.	WF1	AF1	Acc.	WF1	AF1
HC	88.74	88.32	58.93	89.96	89.53	63.76	90.38	89.98	64.87
CBH	88.99	88.23	58.20	89.66	88.99	62.27	89.30	88.81	61.99
CBS	89.61	89.07	63.72	90.22	89.88	67.5	90.36	89.96	66.92
MLP	90.79	90.4	66.33	91.11	90.86	68.17	90.94	90.65	66.37
CNN	90.34	89.71	62.10	90.58	90.19	65.26	90.38	89.98	63.38
LSTM	90.88	90.60	67.20	91.29	91.16	69.71	91.33	91.21	68.64
Hybrid	**91.10**	**90.75**	**67.31**	**91.76**	**91.56**	**70.86**	**91.44**	**91.25**	**69.04**
AE	85.88	85.90	49.54	87.80	87.60	55.62	86.84	86.78	52.67

Table 2.7: Performance metrics (in percent) of different feature extraction models on the *OPPORTUNITY* dataset with different window sizes T.

can be noted that, while changing T affects the performances of all models, the best result was obtained in the reference case ($T = 64$). In particular, making the time window larger did not yield better classification performances. This is probably due to the fact that bigger frames potentially contain data related to a higher number of activities, making the majority-labelling strategy employed to annotate the data segments more inaccurate.

2.5 Experimental results on *Uni-MiB SHAR*

This section presents the implementation details of the different feature learning approaches, and the results of their comparative study on the UniMiB-SHAR dataset. The machine specifications for the implementation of all methods remained the same as for the study carried out on the *OPPORTUNITY* dataset.

2.5.1 Implementation details

Most of the feature learning approaches (models and training algorithm) employed on the UniMiB-SHAR data remained unchanged compared to those used on the *OPPORTUNITY* dataset (cf. Section 2.4.1 for details). The only changes concerned model hyper-parameters. For deep-learning-based models, preliminary studies showed that cross-sensor convolutions could improve the classification results (unlike on the *OPPORTUNITY* dataset). For both CNN and Hybrid, only one convolutional block was therefore used, with the convolutional layer performing a cross-sensor convolution. The full list of hyper-parameters is provided in Table 2.8.

For CB, one codebook was constructed by clustering three-dimensional subsequences to consider correlations among different dimensions. In other words, the codebook construction and codeword assignment steps were carried out by regarding each subsequence as a $3w$-dimensional vector. Regarding the hyper-parameter setting, l was set to 1 for dense sampling of subsequences, and the other hyper-parameters were determined as follows: $w = 16$ based on preliminary tests using $\{8, 16, 32, 64, 96\}$, and $N = 2048$ after testing $\{128, 256, 512, 1024, 2048\}$. Because of the high computational cost, a codebook was constructed by applying the k-means clustering to one million randomly selected subsequences. For the soft assignment approach, σ was set to 4 by testing $\{0.25, 0.5, 1, 2, 4, 8, 16, 32\}$.

Model	Parameter	Value
MLP	· # neurons in dense layers 1,2 and 3	6000
CNN	· Conv. kernel size	(32,3)
	· Conv. sliding stride	(1,1)
	· # conv. kernels	100
	· Pool. size	(2,1)
	· # neurons in dense layer	6000
LSTM	· # LSTM cells in layers 1 and 2	151, 151
	· Output dim. of LSTM cells in layers 1 and 2	1000, 1000
	· # neurons in dense layer	6000
Hybrid	· Conv. kernel size	(32,3)
	· Conv. sliding stride	(1,1)
	· # conv. kernels	100
	· Pool. size	(2,1)
	· # LSTM cells in layers 1 and 2	60, 60
	· Output dim. of LSTM cells in layers 1 and 2	1000, 1000
	· # neurons in dense layer	6000
AE	· # neurons in encoder & decoder dense layer	6000

Table 2.8: Hyper-parameters of the deep-learning-based models on the UniMiB-SHAR dataset. The parameter values are given assuming that the input of the models is of size $T \times S$. Convolutional kernels and pooling sizes are respectively given as $(f_T^{(k)}, f_S^{(k)})$ and $(p_T^{(k)}, p_S^{(k)})$ (based on their definition in Section 2.3.2).

2.5.2 Comparative study results

A30-fold Leave-One-Subject-Out cross validation was performed on the UniMiB-SHAR dataset: the data from one subject was used for testing, from the others subjects for training, and the process was then repeated for all of the 30 subjects. Because of the high computational cost of CBH and CBS, only one codebook was constructed using subsequences collected from all 30 subjects, and then used to build features on all folds. Subsequences of test subjects were thus also used for the training on each fold, which might slightly skew CB performances. However, experiments on a simple training/testing partition (20 first subjects/10 last subjects, respectively) presented in Section 2.6 showed that using completely distinct datasets for the codebook construction and evaluation did not change the relative performances of CBS and Hybrid.)

The final performance metrics are the average of those obtained for each subject. The results are provided in Table 2.9. For a baseline comparison, the results obtained by the authors of [104] who directly used the data contained in the time windows as inputs of the classifier (i.e. no feature extraction) were also added.

Method	Accuracy	Weighted F1-score	Average F1-score
Baseline [104]	54.70	—	—
HC	32.01	22.85	13.78
CBH	75.21	74.13	60.01
CBS	**77.03**	**75.93**	63.23
MLP	71.62	70.81	59.97
CNN	74.97	74.29	**64.65**
LSTM	71.47	70.82	59.32
Hybrid	74.63	73.65	64.47
AE	65.67	64.84	55.04

Table 2.9: Thirty-fold Leave-One-Subject-Out cross validation performance metrics (in percent) of the different feature extraction models on the UniMiB-SHAR dataset.

The codebook approach with soft-assignments yielded the highest accuracy and weighted F1-score at 77.03% and 75.93% respectively, while the the best average F1-score was obtained by CNN at 64.65%. Overall, CBS, CNN and Hybrid yield sensibly better performances than the other feature extraction methods. This might in part be caused by the specific segmentation technique employed on this dataset: since data frames are exclusively centred around peaks of input signals, local features characterising the shape of the peaks - typically obtained by codebook approaches and ANNs containing convolutional layers - carry a high relevance to the classification problem. The lack of temporal consistency between the different data frames or the absence of frames characterising transitions between different actions might explain the relatively poor performances displayed by the LSTM architecture.

2.6 Overall analysis

The results obtained on both datasets highlight three points: the superiority of automatically learned features over hand-crafted ones, the stability of hybrid CNN-LSTM architectures which are able to obtain top performing features on both datasets, and the relevance of the codebook approach with soft-assignment to some specific setups.

If the bad results obtained by hand-crafted features compared to the other feature learning approaches are not unexpected, the gap in their relative performances displayed on both datasets is more surprising: the difference between their average F1-score and the one of the best performing method is 7.39% on *OPPORTUNITY*, and 49.93% on UniMiB-SHAR. To investigate this, a Robust Feature Selection (RFS) method [153] was applied to determine which features were the most relevant to the classification problem. On *OPPORTUNITY*, the best features were acquired by sensors placed on the feet of the subjects. It is hypothesised that this is due to the fact that the dominant NULL class on *OPPORTUNITY* mainly comprises transitions of the subjects between two different locations of the experimental environment, whereas the other ADLs featured in the dataset do not involve any significant movement of the lower part of the body. Sensors placed on the feet of the subjects and their associated features would then be effective to distinguish the NULL class from the others. On the other hand, the lack of dominant class coupled to the specific peak shape of the signals explains the low performance on the UniMiB-SHAR dataset, as well as its inferiority to the baseline raw data approach.

One interesting observation is the dependence of the performances of deep learning models on the segmentation phase. Depending on whether the latter is sliding-window-based (e.g., *OPPORTUNITY*) or energy-based (e.g., UniMiB-SHAR), the type of data frames varies, thus impacting the type of predominant features for the classification. Features characterising the shape of the time signals - which are typically obtained by convolution-based networks - perform well in the case of an energy-based segmentation, whereas a sliding window segmentation approach makes the memorisation of previous data frames and the LSTM-based architectures more relevant. It can be noted that the hybrid CNN and LSTM model still ranks among the most efficient methods on UniMiB-SHAR, which highlights the stability of this model, and suggests its good generalisation capacity on different datasets.

2.7 Summary

Section 2 presented the results of a comparative study of various state-of-the-art feature extraction approaches in a context of sensor-based HAR. Eight feature extraction methods including feature engineering, unsupervised and supervised feature learning were compared on two benchmark datasets: *OPPORTUNITY* and UniMiB-SHAR. In order to provide a comparison in the fairest conditions, a specific evaluation framework fixing all steps of the ARC - except for feature extraction - was defined. The results of the study highlighted the following main points:

- Feature learning approaches outperformed the traditional feature engineering approach on both datasets, confirming trends reported in various evaluation setups in the literature [130, 133, 136, 138, 9].

- Feature learning using supervised deep learning yielded the best performances on both datasets. The good performances of convolutional and recurrent networks with LSTM cells for sensor-based HAR were in particular highlighted. Models using LSTM layers obtained top performances on *OPPORTUNITY* while models with convolutional layers returned the best performances on *UniMIB-SHAR*. Hybrid architectures combining both types of layers performed consistently good on both datasets which confirms other similar observations in the literature [9]. On the other hand, feature learning using unsupervised deep learning (autoencoders) did not yield as good results - which follows a trend highlighted in [138] - and was outperformed by feature engineering on *OPPORTUNITY*.

- Despite being much less popular than deep learning, feature learning not using DNNs (i.e. codebook approaches) performed well overall, ranking among the top methods on *UniMIB-SHAR* in particular. The lower popularity of such feature learning methods could potentially be attributed to their sensibility to variations in hyper-parameters (e.g. subsequence length, number of codewords) which forces the determination of an optimal set of parameters using time-consuming methods such as grid search, and makes their training more complex overall [142].

The overall results of this comparative study highlight the strong potential of DNNs for feature learning in the context of sensor-based HAR. It should however be noted that this observation does not necessarily translate to other application fields of ubiquitous computing. The popularity of sensor-based HAR among the ubiquitous computing community and the relative simplicity of acquiring human movement data has led to a relative abundance of labelled data as evidenced by the large number of available datasets in multiple application contexts. Such a trend is not necessarily observed for other applications, which can make the use of feature learning approaches more difficult. In those configurations, it is necessary to use specific techniques to bypass data scarcity such as transfer learning [44]. The following Sections will provide an overview of how to apply such methods in a time-series classification context, and present the deep transfer learning approach proposed in the frame of this thesis.

Chapter 3

Deep transfer learning based on sensor modality discrimination

3.1 Problem statement

In this Section, the motivations and challenges behind deep transfer learning for time-series data are firstly presented. An overview of transfer learning in a general context and *deep transfer learning* - i.e. transfer learning applied to DNNs - is then provided.

3.1.1 Motivation

The prevalence of wearable devices has simplified the collection of sensor data for ubiquitous and wearable computing applications over the past years. In this context, machine learning has become necessary to provide meaningful services by automatically recognising complex patterns in time-series data. Following the most common approach, an ubiquitous computing application - like sensor-based HAR or Emotion Recognition (ER) - is formulated into a classification problem. A classification model is built on a training dataset composed of sensor data labelled with their corresponding classes (e.g. activities and emotions for HAR and ER, respectively). The model is then used to estimate the class of test data whose actual class is unknown.

Getting a proper abstracted representation of the data - i.e. features - is essential to obtain satisfying recognition performances for a given problem. Already illustrated in Chapter 2 in the context of HAR, this paradigm has been shown to remain valid for other application domains involving time-series data [154]. In traditional approaches and no matter the considered application, features were heuristically engineered based on prior knowledge about sensor data in the target problem. They have however been progressively overshadowed by *feature learning* methods, which learn useful features on data in a more automated way [155, 10], and whose most notable and popular example nowadays is deep learning. The effectiveness of DNNs has been consistently verified over the past years for numerous wearable-computing applications, including HAR as illustrated in Chapter 2 and ER [156, 157].

Using DNNs is, however, confronted with several difficulties in practice, such as lack of practical technique for the optimisation of hyper-parameters (e.g. neural activation function, number of layers, number of neurons per layer, etc.), requirements in high computational power to train complex models in a reasonable amount of time, etc. Among them, the major obstacle remains the need for a large quantity of labelled training data. A high diversity in the training data is required so that the classification model becomes robust to the intra-class variability which might be caused by many different factors. For HAR for instance, a way to execute a certain activity may significantly vary depending on persons, producing very different sensor data. Even the same person could produce intra-class variability by performing the same activity in different ways due to external factors (e.g. surrounding environment, positions of sensors, etc).

A possible solution to alleviate the data scarcity problem is *transfer learning*, which refers to techniques that aim at extracting knowledge from a *source domain*, and using it to improve the learning of a model on a *target domain* [44]. Data from the source domain can partially compensate the scarcity of data on the target domain. In other words, by performing some specific *task* on the source domain, the model can learn information relevant to the target problem on "external" data. *Deep transfer learning* - which refers to transfer learning applied to DNNs - has in particular become widespread with the rise in popularity of DNNs. Typically, parameters (weights and biases) of a DNN pre-trained on a source domain are transferred to another compatible DNN on the target domain. Previous works have shown that the success of the gradient descent optimisation applied during the training of a DNN is heavily dependent on the initial values of its parameters [20]. Deep transfer learning is based on the assumption that if the features learned on the source domain are also useful for the target domain, then the parameters of a DNN pre-trained on the source domain are also adequate initial parameters for a DNN on the target domain [45, 46]. Once transferred, the target DNN is *fine-tuned*, i.e. retrained using the target data to adjust the transferred parameters to the problem on the target domain as needed.

On the one hand, using transfer learning has become standard when image modalities are involved. Very large datasets containing images representing a large variety of objects - such as ImageNet - have led to obtaining powerful DNN models (e.g. AlexNet, VGG-net, etc.) trained for image classification or object detection. It was shown that their weights encode general and powerful object-related features [32] which could lead to performance improvements when transferred to a DNN for solving a specific target task. On the other hand, transfer learning has not reached the same level of maturity when time-series data are involved for several reasons. Firstly, time-series data are rather scarce due to the high cost of the labelling task for a specific application. This results in a lack of very large-scale time-series datasets (like ImageNet for images). Secondly, the development of a transfer learning method working for any type of time-series data is confronted with the difficulty that data formats on the target domain can significantly vary depending on the application. Some sensors can for instance provide "sparse" time-series containing data points unevenly spaced in time indicating events, while others provide "non-sparse" time-series consisting of data values evenly spaced in time and sampled at high frequencies. Additionally, two distinct applications of ubiquitous computing may use different numbers and types of sensors because of differences in the relevance of devices, their obtrusiveness or easiness to setup, etc. Those applications thus rely on data consisting of different numbers of *channels*, where we refer to a *channel* as one dimension of a sequence of sensor recordings (e.g. a temperature sensor provides a single channel sequence, while 3-axis accelerometers record three channels, each indicating the acceleration on one axis). This is especially important in the context of deep transfer learning because differences in number of sensor channels can lead to different DNN architectures on the source and target domains - since the architecture of a DNN is impacted by the shape of its input data - thus making transfers of weights more complicated.

While deep time-series transfer learning is a research question which has been explored in the past, the aforementioned obstacles have led to limitations in the approaches proposed in the literature. To avoid issues related to differences in data formats between source and target datasets, many studies decided to restrain their scope by adding strong similarity conditions between source and target domains (e.g. same type of data, same classes, etc.) and focusing on specific applications such as sensor-based HAR [48, 49, 50]. Other studies attempting to provide transfer methods for time-series with a more general scope (i.e. with fewer restrictions on source and target domains) [51, 158] have focused exclusively on the case where single-channel data are involved. While this allowed them to bypass the problem of handling different numbers of sensor channels in the source and target domains, it also limited their scopes since multi-channel time-series data are often encountered in real-life applications.

In this context, an attempt to find a deep transfer learning method for multi-channel time-series data was made in the frame of this thesis. A deep transfer learning method for time-series is proposed that leverages existing datasets to bypass the issue of data scarcity on the target domain. Studies are carried out using non-sparse time-series datasets because they are the most common type of data in ubiquitous computing applications. Transfer learning for images has shown that learning general image features on ImageNet led to successful transfer of information on various target domains. In a similar way, the proposed approach aims at learning general features for non-sparse time-series data which could be re-purposed to various target domains. It hinges on the hypothesis that learning features related to the type of time-series data could be an appropriate proxy task to achieve this goal. We therefore propose to use *sensor modalities* as labels, which are commonly available. Two sensors are considered to be part of the same modality group if they measure the same type of measurement, and perform it in similar ways. For instance, similar devices acquiring acceleration placed at different locations are part of the same sensor modality group; acceleration acquired from two different types of devices are considered as different sensor modalities (measurement processed in different ways); acceleration and EEG are considered as different modalities (different types of measurements). The proposed transfer method is designed so that it can be applied to other target domains involving any number of channels. It firstly decomposes data on a source domain into single-channel data, and trains a DNN called *single-channel DNN (sDNN)* for sensor-modality classification. Then, a model called *multichannel DNN (mDNN)* [154] is built by replicating and fine-tuning the sDNN for each of the channels on the target domain. This mDNN performs recognition on the target domain by fusing outputs from all channels.

In the next Sections, a more detailed description of transfer learning is firstly provided. A review of related works in the past literature is then performed to identify existing solutions and compare them to the proposed transfer approach in this thesis. The method is then described in detail, and experimental results and their analysis are finally discussed.

3.1.2 Transfer learning

Definition and challenges

Transfer learning is a subset of machine learning which encompasses techniques aiming to enhance the performances of a specific problem using knowledge learned by solving a different - but usually related - problem. Initially introduced for neural networks in the early 1990s [159], transfer learning rose to popularity over the past years after converging evidence of its beneficial effects on the training of models in various frameworks was observed [7, 5]. This trend led to an increased diversity in types of proposed transfer learning approaches in the literature, using different types of data, models or strategies to transfer knowledge. Transfer learning has nowadays become state-of-the-art in some application fields, in particular those using image modalities such as image classification and segmentation, or object detection in images [5, 46].

Following the multiplication of the proposed approaches, attempts to provide a standardisation of transfer learning concepts have been made to make their understanding easier. The most prominent and widely adopted one is Pan et al. [44], which provided standard definitions to key transfer learning concepts. In particular, the terms of *source domain* referring to the dataset and associated task(s) to learn the knowledge to be transferred, and *target domain* referring to the dataset and associated task(s) to be solved with the help of the transferred knowledge were introduced.

As highlighted in [44], three fundamental questions must be answered before applying a transfer learning approach:

1. **What to transfer?** i.e. what is the format of the transferred knowledge?

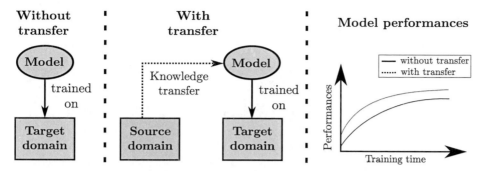

Figure 3.1: Regular machine learning (left) and transfer learning (middle): knowledge is extracted from a source domain and fed to a model trained to solve a task on a target domain. When performed under the proper conditions, transfer learning leads to better performances for the target task compared to where no transfer was used.

2. **How to transfer?** i.e. what type of algorithm can be used to transfer the knowledge from source to target?

3. **When to transfer?** i.e. how to identify situations where transfer would be beneficial and those where it would not be given one or several source domains and one target domain?

The answers to the two first questions are very dependent on the available source and target domains. Parameters such as whether the source and target tasks are the same or not, or whether the source and target data have the same format may have a large impact on how the transfer is performed. To make the identification of a specific transfer learning technique easier, [44] proposed a broad classification of approaches into three categories: *inductive transfer learning*, which refers to the case where source and target tasks are different, *transductive transfer learning*, when source and target tasks are the same while source and target datasets are different, and *unsupervised transfer learning*, which is a sub-case of inductive transfer learning with an unsupervised target task. As the proposed transfer learning approach in this thesis is part of the inductive transfer family, a more detailed description of these types of approaches will be performed in the following Sections.

Finally, it can be noted that the answer to the third question (on when to perform transfer) is still an open research question without clear answers for now. Many past publications have investigated the question of knowing which source domain(s) would be the most adapted for transfer to a given target domain. Examples can be found for image classification and segmentation [160], unimodal time-series classification [158] or sensor-based HAR [48]. Existing studies have, however, been mostly carried out on specific application domains, and the lack of fundamental research on this question has not allowed clear and cross-applications answers to emerge for now. In particular, one notable finding highlighted in past works which still remains unexplained is that transfer between a seemingly unrelated source and target domain could - counter-intuitively - yield a good boost in performances for the target task [46, 158].

Inductive transfer

Inductive transfer learning (i.e. different source and target tasks) represents one of the most commonly encountered forms of transfer learning in practice. The more specific a target task is, the less likely that other similar datasets to the target one (e.g. data coming from the same sensors, same labels) are available to perform transfer learning. In those conditions, the main options become to select either a source domain that is only loosely related to the target one, or a dataset large enough to allow the learning of generic features (e.g ImageNet for image related transfer learning [5, 46]).

The prevalence of inductive transfer learning has led to a large variety in proposed approaches in many application contexts. To help with their identification, [44] provides a finer-grained categorisation of inductive transfer learning techniques based on how the transfer of knowledge is performed:

- **Transfer of instances** refers to techniques attempting to directly re-use subsets of the source domain to train models for the target task. Such approaches usually assume that some minimum conditions of similarity between the source and target data (e.g. same type of data or same labels) are fulfilled.

- **Transfer of feature representations** includes techniques attempting to find a "good" feature representation which would be suitable for both source and target tasks on their respective datasets. This category of approaches usually works under the assumption that the source and target tasks are related, and has close ties with Multi-Task Learning [161].

- **Transfer of parameters** refers to approaches training a model to solve the source task on the source domain, then transferring its parameters to a similar model to be trained to solve the target task on the target domain. The assumption that both models used to process the source and target tasks are similar must be verified to apply this type of transfer.

- **Transfer of relational knowledge** designates a type of transfer approaches that can be applied on "relational" source and target domains, i.e. on domains with datasets where each data point has a known relationship with others (e.g. social network data). Those methods focus on transferring relationships among the source data to the target dataset.

It can be noted that the past years have seen a sharp rise in proposed approaches using transfer of parameters, due to the increasing popularity of deep learning, the good performances exhibited by transfer learning for DNNs - in particular for tasks involving image modalities [5, 46] - and the relative simplicity of transferring neural weights and biases from one architecture to another.

Transfer learning applied to deep-neural networks

Transfer learning for DNNs falls into the category of transfer of parameters approaches, with the transferred parameters being the neural weights and biases. It is traditionally performed in four steps:

1. **Training of the source DNN:** a specific DNN architecture - the *source DNN* - is defined to solve the source task, and then trained on the source dataset.

2. **Definition of the target DNN:** a *target DNN* is defined to solve the target task, with some or all of its layers copying the ones of the source DNN. This condition is necessary to guarantee that the sizes of the weight matrices and bias vectors between at least one pair of two consecutive layers remain invariant between source and target DNNs.

3. **Transfer of weights:** the learned weights and bias of the layers in the source DNN are transferred to the corresponding associated layers of the target DNN.

4. **Fine-tuning:** the target DNN is trained on the target domain, leading to the transferred weights to be re-adapted for the target task.

The practical implementation of those steps mostly varies depending on the considered application field. For applications involving image modalities such as image classification and segmentation, it has become common practice to re-use the N first layers of very deep benchmark DNNs trained for image classification on ImageNet [3] such as AlexNet [143], VGG-Net [36], GoogLeNet [162], etc., with $N \in \mathcal{N}^*$ parameter empirically determined which depends on the considered target problem. For applications involving other modalities - such as time-series data - the lack of benchmark DNNs has led to a higher diversity in the application of the four aforementioned steps, and a lack of standardisation for the transfer process.

The effectiveness of transfer of parameters for DNNs is hypothesised to be attributed to two factors. The first is the importance of the initialisation of weights and bias to properly train a deep learning architecture. Studies carried out by Glorot et al. [20] showed that improper or random weight and bias initialisation in simple MLPs for image classification could lead the loss optimisation process to be stuck in suboptimal local minima during the training phase. When performed under the proper conditions, transfer learning allows the target model to be trained with suitable initial parameters, and causes the loss function to head towards better local minima during the training process [5]. The second factor stems from the strong performances of DNNs as feature learners: past works in various application domains such as image classification [32] or speech recognition [163] showed that each neuron in a DNN encodes a specific feature computed on the input of the layer it belongs to, and that the level of abstraction of the feature increases the deeper the layer is. In this context, the transfer of parameters between two DNNs can also be seen as a transfer of features between the source and target domains. A source and target task admitting similar optimal features can increase the chances of the transfer being successful.

3.2 Related work

In this Section, an overview of the most relevant transfer learning approaches applied to DNNs in the literature is performed. Major differences in proposed approaches can be observed among past works depending on what type of data is processed, especially between images and time-series. In this Section, an overview of transfer learning in the image processing field is firstly performed. Transfer learning methods proposed for DNNs taking time-series data as inputs are then reviewed.

3.2.1 Deep transfer learning for image modalities

Most general deep transfer learning methods with proven effectiveness have been developed for image modalities, due to the availability of large datasets like ImageNet [3] (more than 14 million images labelled with over 20,000 different categories). Powerful feature extractor models like AlexNet [143], VGG-net [36] and ResNet [164] were trained on subsets of the ImageNet dataset in the frame of the ImageNet Large Scale Visual Recognition Challenges (ILSVRC) and are nowadays regularly re-used and fine-tuned for more specific applications [46]. The first studies hinting at the benefits of transfer learning emerged approximately at the same time. In [32] a key aspect of the behaviour of Convolutional Neural Networks (CNNs) was highlighted by showing that each neuron of convolutional layers encodes a specific feature, whose specificity increases with the depth of the layer using a variant of AlexNet [143]. The authors also analysed the generality of features learned by the model trained on the source domain (ImageNet) by checking its transferability on three smaller target domains. The major performance improvements showed the potential of parameter-based transfers for DNNs. In a similar fashion, [5] managed to show how AlexNet could improve the performances of various target problems such as domain adaptation, object recognition, sub-category and scene recognition. The authors of [7] trained a variant of AlexNet for image classification, and transferred it for object detection and localisation tasks, obtaining state-of-the-art results in both setups. In [165], the authors extracted features from warped regions of images by pre-training a variant of AlexNet on a subset of ImageNet. It was then fine-tuned using the warped images as inputs for image classification on two different target domains (PASCAL VOC and a different subset of ImageNet). The transferred model was able to significantly outperform the previously best solutions on both target domains. Similarly, [6] presented a study in which the layers of AlexNet trained on ImageNet were transferred to a DNN model designed for object and action classification on the PASCAL VOC dataset. In [45], researchers analysed the impact of different transfer learning parameters for AlexNet such as number of transferred layers, using fine-tuning or not, using different subsets of

ImageNet as source and target. They showed that the target performance drops when only transferring deeper layers (which were shown to encode features more specific to the source problem [32]), and how important fine-tuning on the target domain was. In addition, it was demonstrated that the transfer learning process could boost the generalisation capacity of the network compared to not using it.

All the aforementioned works greatly contributed to making transfer learning state-of-the-art when working with DNNs processing images. In the wake of this, attempts to improve its efficiency by playing on parameters not related to the DNN architecture were made, such as trying to optimise the source domain selection for a given target domain. The authors of [160] presented a method based on information theory to reach this goal. Assuming that different CNNs with similar architectures have each been trained on a source domain, they proposed a ranking metric called "transferability" by computing the Mutual Information between the target labels and the features of each of the CNNs. The transferability can be used to estimate how much a specific source domain can reduce the uncertainty in predicting the test labels. Experiments showed that the top ranked CNNs in terms of transferability led to the best performances after transfer and fine-tuning on the target domain. In [166], a search engine to find relevant image source datasets given a target domain was proposed. First, a data server that contains three publicly available image datasets for various applications (e.g. face recognition, self-driving cars, generic image classification) with various associated tasks (either supervised or unsupervised) was built. Each source dataset was then partitioned into non-overlapping subsets by applying k-means clustering on the features of a DNN pre-trained on ImageNet. On each partition, rotated versions of the images it contains were created and a model - referred to as *expert* - was trained for a proxy task involving image rotation classification. A *Mixture of Experts (MoE)* model taking into account all experts trained on the partition of a source dataset was finally defined to represent the latter. The proposed search engine finally indicated the source datasets whose MoE performed the best for the proxy task on the target dataset as best suggestions to perform the transfer. Experiments carried out for seven target domains with tasks including either classification, detection or instance segmentation showed that the optimal source datasets retrieved by the search engine could lead to consistent improvement in performances after transfer compared to no transfer.

Directions explored to enhance transfer learning also include attempts to improve the fine-tuning performances on the target dataset. Assuming that a pre-trained model is available on a source domain (e.g. ImageNet), the authors of [167] proposed to jointly train a "policy network" using a Gumbel Softmax distribution and a DNN for the target classification task. For each testing image and layer of the target DNN, the policy network is used to determine whether the weights of the layer should be frozen or fine-tuned using the image. Experiments showed that the proposed adaptive fine-tuning approach led to better results than other state-of-the-art fine-tuning and regularisation techniques. In [168], Li et al. investigated the effectiveness of different regularisation approaches whose aim is to keep the weights which are fine-tuned on the target domain as close as possible to those learned on the source domain. A baseline consisting of a regular fine-tuning of the target DNN was also tested. Experiments for image classification and segmentation showed that all regularisation approaches led to better performances than the baseline.

As final remark: all transfer learning works that were presented in this Section are based on the supervised pre-training of one or several DNN models on a source domain. Unsupervised pre-training using unlabelled data was also attempted for image modalities [46, 169], but failed to yield performances as good as supervised pre-training regardless of the quantity of available unlabelled data.

3.2.2 Deep transfer learning for time-series

Transfer learning techniques have so far been much less explored for time-series data because of the scarcity of data in the ubiquitous computing field, and the absence of a large-scale labelled dataset like ImageNet. As a result, most past works have attempted to propose transfer methods that work only for specific applications. Due to its relatively higher abundance of available data, sensor-based HAR has in particular been more extensively explored than other applications of ubiquitous computing. In [48], the results in several scenarios of parameter transfer such as transfer between subjects, datasets, sensor localisation or modalities were presented. All transferred models were tested against a baseline that regularly trains the model on the target domain only. Despite poor relative performances of the transferred models compared to the baseline, the study highlighted some interesting phenomena, such as the fact that the transfer performances were sensibly better when parameters of only the first layers were transferred. [49] presented a transfer approach for CNN when labelled target data are scarce, but labelled source data are available. It firstly trains a CNN using labelled data on the source domain and defines a CNN with similar architecture on the target domain. The target CNN is then trained on unlabelled data to minimise the distance between its parameters and the ones of the source CNN. It however only works under the assumption that the set of activities on the source and target domains is the same. In [50], an iterative co-training approach using classification models trained on labelled source data to attribute pseudo-labels to unlabelled target data was presented. It works under the assumption that source and target domains contain the same labels. A transformation which minimises the maximum mean discrepancy between labelled and pseudo-labelled examples is found. Source and target data are then projected into a common space using the transformation, and classifiers are trained on the projected data to attribute more reliable labels.

In addition to being limited to sensor-based HAR, all aforementioned studies can only be applied assuming strict conditions on the similarity between source and target domains (e.g. same set of labels, same type of data, etc.), thus limiting their scope. To the best of our knowledge, only two past works proposed a general transfer learning method that is potentially usable for different ubiquitous computing applications. In [51], a Recurrent Neural Network (RNN) was trained using data from the UCR Time Series Classification Archive (UCRTSCA)[170] that consists of 85 small-scale univariate time-series datasets covering a wide range of sensor modalities, such as accelerometer data, energy demand, chemical concentration in water, etc. The RNN composed of an encoder and decoder was trained to reproduce its input on its output layer using a subset of 24 datasets of the UCRTSCA (source domain). After this pre-training step, the encoder was used as a feature extractor for a Support Vector Machine (SVM) fine-tuned on each of 30 other datasets of the UCRTSCA (target domain). The experimental results indicated that data on source domains not necessarily related to the target domain was still useful for achieving state-of-the-art results. In [158], a method to compute the similarity between source and target datasets to determine the most suitable dataset for transfer was proposed. It assumes that one labelled target and several labelled source datasets are available. For each dataset, the method firstly computes the average of sequences for each class using Dynamic Time Warping Barycentre Averaging (DBA). The average of all class averages is then computed with DBA to yield a "characteristic sequence" of the dataset. The similarity between two datasets is computed using the Dynamic Time Warping (DTW) distance between their respective characteristic sequences. The source dataset with the lowest distance is then chosen and used to train a DNN. Its weights are finally transferred on the target domain for fine-tuning. Experiments carried out on the 85 datasets of the UCRTSCA showed that the transfer yielded better classification performances when the similarity between source and target was higher.

Despite their more general scope than other time-series transfer approaches, the methods in [51] and [158] remain limited to the case of processing single-channel sequences since their experiments were both carried out on the UCRTSCA. General transfer learning for multichannel time-series is a more challenging problem since differences in the number of sensor channels between the source and target domains can lead to differences in DNN architectures to process the source and target tasks (thus breaking the assumption on the similarity between source and target models required for a transfer of parameters). In this thesis, an approach for multichannel time-series transfer learning with a general scope is proposed and described in the following Sections.

3.3 Sensor modality discrimination for deep transfer learning

While deep transfer learning for time-series has been explored in the past literature, the scope of the proposed approaches has so far been limited, which constrain their application in practice. On the one hand, some methods from the literature can only be applied under strict conditions on the similarity between source and target domains, such as data coming from the same sensors or same type of labels on the source and target datasets. Such constraints drastically reduce the number of suitable choices for a source domain given a specific target domain, thus making their application difficult for cases in which publicly available data are scarce (e.g. sensor-based ER). On the other hand, the few attempts to propose a transfer approach which would work without constraints of similarity between source and target domains have been limited only to cases where single-channel data were used [51, 158]. In this context, a time-series transfer learning approach proposing a solution to those limitations was introduced in [102]. The following Section describes it in detail.

3.3.1 Methodology

Using the notations of [44] and [171], a *labelled domain dataset* $\mathcal{D}$ is defined as a combination of two components: one set of data instances $\mathcal{X}$ and a vector of associated labels $\mathcal{Y}$. A *task* $\mathcal{T}$ is defined as the association of $\mathcal{Y}$ with a *predictive function* f to be learned from the labelled data. The source and target domains datasets are referred to as $\mathcal{D}_S = \{\mathcal{X}_S, \mathcal{Y}_S\}$ and $\mathcal{D}_T = \{\mathcal{X}_T, \mathcal{Y}_T\}$, while the source and target tasks are denoted by $\mathcal{T}_S = \{\mathcal{Y}_S, f_S\}$ and $\mathcal{T}_T = \{\mathcal{Y}_T, f_T\}$, respectively. It is assumed that $\mathcal{T}_T$ and $\mathcal{D}_T$ - which respectively represent the target ubiquitous computing problem to solve and its associated labelled dataset - are available.

A *deep transfer learning* strategy based on transferring DNN weights learned on a sensor-modality classification problem on $\mathcal{D}_S$ to another DNN trained to solve $\mathcal{T}_T$ on $\mathcal{D}_T$ is proposed. The method - illustrated in Figure 3.2 - belongs to the category of *inductive transfers*, since the source and target tasks are different ($\mathcal{T}_S \neq \mathcal{T}_T$). It consists of the following steps:

1. **Building of $\mathcal{D}_S$ and $\mathcal{T}_S$:** $\mathcal{X}_S$ is firstly built by considering M multichannel time-series datasets. Every multichannel sequence in the jth dataset ($1 \leqslant j \leqslant M$) is decomposed into individual channels, each of which is divided into *segments* of length L using a sliding window approach. The segments are aggregated to form the source dataset $\mathcal{X}_S$ defined in Equation 3.1:

$$\mathcal{X}_S = \bigcup_{j=1}^{M} \{x_i^{(j)} \in \mathbb{R}^L \,|\, 1 \leqslant i \leqslant N_j\} \qquad (3.1)$$

   where $x_i^{(j)}$ refers to the ith segment of the jth source dataset, and N_j is the total number of segments obtained from the jth source dataset. In other words, $\mathcal{X}_S$ is the union of all segments extracted from the M source datasets. The source task $\mathcal{T}_S$ is defined as the classification of sensor modalities on $\mathcal{D}_S$. Sensor modality labels $\mathcal{Y}_S$ are defined by the following Equation 3.2:

$$\mathcal{Y}_S = \bigcup_{j=1}^{M} \{y_i^{(j)} \in \{1, 2, \ldots, C_S\} \,|\, 1 \leqslant i \leqslant N_j\} \qquad (3.2)$$

where C_S is the number of sensor modalities (i.e. classes) of the source domain, and $y_i^{(j)}$ indicates the sensor modality of $x_i^{(j)} \in \mathcal{X}_S$. f_S is the function which attributes each $x_i^{(j)}$ to its corresponding sensor modality $y_i^{(j)}$.

2. **Learning of f_S:** A single-channel DNN (sDNN) is used to learn f_S, as shown in Figure 3.2 (a). For the sDNN architecture, a batch normalisation layer is used to perform a regularisation on the segments in $\mathcal{X}_S$ to address the issue of the heterogeneity of the source data. Assuming the sDNN contains $H \in \mathbb{N}^*$ hidden layers, we denote the weight matrix and bias vector of the kth layer ($1 \leqslant k \leqslant H$) as W_k and b_k, respectively. Finally, a softmax layer with C_S neurons is added, with each neuron of the layer outputting a value which is an estimation of probability to its corresponding class. This way, the sDNN can classify the segments of $\mathcal{X}_S$ using the labels $\mathcal{Y}_S$.

3. **Initialisation of a multichannel DNN (mDNN):** A mDNN is defined to learn f_T, as shown in Figure 3.3. It is trained using $\mathcal{X}_T$ which contains multichannel segments $X \in \mathbb{R}^{L \times S}$, with S being the number of channels of the target dataset and $\mathcal{Y}_T$ which contains associated labels $Y \in \{1, 2, \ldots, C_T\}$ with C_T being the number of classes of the target problem. For the mDNN architecture, a batch normalisation layer is applied to the segments to perform an operation akin to a standard normalisation on the input of the network. The S sensor channels are then separated. The sth sensor channel ($1 \leqslant s \leqslant S$) is processed by an ensemble of hidden layers of the same number and type as the hidden layers of the sDNN. This ensemble of layers is referred to as a *branch* of the mDNN, as depicted in Figure 3.3. The output of each branch is then concatenated and connected to fully-connected layers. A softmax layer with C_T neurons is then added to output class probabilities for the C_T target classes.

4. **Transfer of weights from the sDNN to the mDNN:** The weights W_k and biases b_k of the H hidden layers of the sDNN[1] learned on $\{\mathcal{D}_S, \mathcal{T}_S\}$ are transferred to the branches of the mDNN, as shown in Figure 3.3. In other words, the kth layer of the sth branch (for $1 \leqslant k \leqslant H$ and $1 \leqslant s \leqslant S$) has its weight and bias matrices $W_k^{(s)}$ and $b_k^{(s)}$ initialised as W_k and b_k, respectively.

5. **Learning of f_T:** The mDNN is fined-tuned using $(\mathcal{X}_T, \mathcal{Y}_T)$ to learn f_T, which is the predictive function for the target ubiquitous computing problem.

3.3.2 Implementation details

While the proposed approach can be applied regardless of the type of layers chosen for the sDNN and branches of the mDNN, CNNs were used in the following studies because of their good performances for time-series classification in diverse application fields of ubiquitous computing [158]. The proposed transfer approach is therefore referred to as *CNN-transfer* from now on. Fully-connected and recurrent

---

[1] Weights and biases of batch normalisation and softmax layers of the sDNN are not transferred.

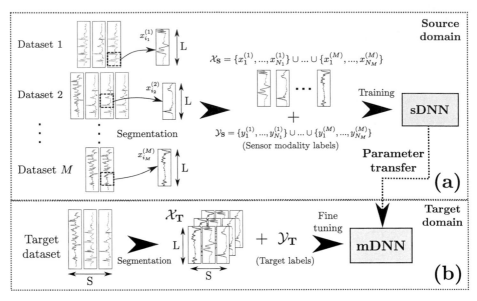

Figure 3.2: An overview of the proposed time-series transfer learning method. (a) A labelled source dataset of single-channel sequences $(\mathcal{X}_S, \mathcal{Y}_S)$ is created by collecting segments $x_i^{(j)}$ of length L from M datasets and attributing them sensor modality labels $y_i^{(j)}$. $(\mathcal{X}_S, \mathcal{Y}_S)$ is then used to train a sDNN that predicts the sensor modality of each segment. (b) A mDNN is built to learn the predictive target function f_T. The weights of the trained sDNN are transferred to the mDNN. The latter is then fine-tuned on the target domain using $(\mathcal{X}_T, \mathcal{Y}_T)$.

layers with Long-Short-Term-Memory (LSTM) cells were also tested for hidden layers of the sDNNs. But both of them ended up performing worse than convolutional layers in all configurations. Those results are consistent with past works which showed that CNNs are better feature extractors than fully-connected or LSTM networks in a time-series classification context [172]. For LSTM-based architectures in particular, finding a properly performing baseline architecture (i.e. not using any transfer) on the target datasets ended up being impractical. The high number of LSTM parameters and the large size of our multichannel architecture limited the complexity of the tested mDNN. In addition, using multichannel data segments with long temporal length significantly extended the training time of LSTM models (based on the backpropagation-through-time algorithm) compared to CNN-based approaches (even in configurations where simple LSTM architectures were tested), and increased the likelihood to overfit. Both phenomena were already highlighted in past HAR literature [8] and comforted our decision to use CNNs in our experiments.

Four datasets taken from the UCI machine learning repository [173] were used in our study to build the source domain, covering 16 different sensor modalities in total: *OPPORTUNITY* [103] (accelerometers and IMUs data for Activities of Daily Life recognition), *gas-mixture* [174] (gas concentration and conductance chemical

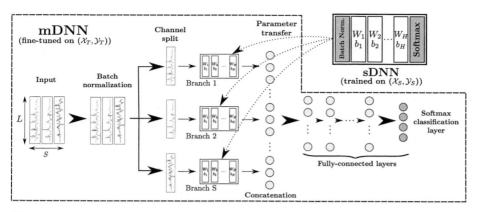

Figure 3.3: mDNN used for the learning of f_T on the target domain. The input segments of the target dataset $\mathcal{X}_T$ are sent through a batch normalisation layer. All sensor channels are then separated and processed by S branches with the same number and type of hidden layers as the sDNN trained on the source dataset $(\mathcal{X}_S, \mathcal{Y}_S)$. The outputs of the S branches are concatenated and sent through fully-connected and softmax layers for classification. The mDNN is fine-tuned using the target dataset $(\mathcal{X}_T, \mathcal{Y}_T)$.

sensor readings data), *EEG-eye-state* [175] (ElectroEncophaloGraphy (EEG) data for open/close eye recognition) and *energy-appliance* [176] (data from a low-energy house such as temperature, humidity, air pressure, energy consumption for the prediction of energy consumption). Each dataset contains multi-channel data with numbers of channels ranging from 14 to 107 channels. $C_S = 16$ sensor modalities were obtained in total by using the documentation and information provided by the authors of each dataset. A sDNN trained on the source domain therefore had a softmax layer with 16 units, each outputting the probability that a segment belongs to one sensor modality. The complete list of modalities in the source domain is provided in Table 3.1.

It should be noted that OPPORTUNITY and gas-mixture are notably larger than the other datasets. The question of balancing the source datasets therefore arose. Two approaches were tested: one downsampling the largest dataset so that all datasets provide a balanced contribution, the other taking as much data as possible from each dataset. Both approaches yielded comparable performances, in accordance with a similar analysis where the quantity of data to train transferred models is changed [46]. The best performances attained by the aforementioned two approaches are reported in the following Sections.

In order to test the effectiveness of the proposed transfer approach, two target datasets belonging to different application fields of wearable computing were used: a newly introduced sensor-based HAR dataset called the *Cognitive Village - MSBand* dataset - referred to as *CogAge dataset* for the sake of simplicity - and the *DEAP* dataset [66], main benchmark for sensor-based ER.

Table 3.1: List of sensor modalities in the source domain using the OPPORTU-NITY, gas-mixture, EEG-Eye-State and energy-appliance datatsets (obtained from the documentation of each respective dataset). The respective units of measurement are provided in parenthesis when the information was available.

Source dataset	Sensor modalities	
OPPORTUNITY	· Acceleration (in milli g)	· IMU EU (in degree)
	· IMU magnetometer	· IMU angular velocity (in $mm.s^{-1}$)
	· IMU gyroscope	· IMU compass (in degree)
	· IMU acceleration (normalised value in milli g)	
gas-mixture	· Gas concentration (in ppm)	· Conductance (in $k\Omega^{-1}$)
EEG-eye-state	· EEG	
energy-appliance	· Energy use (in $W.h^{-1}$)	· Pressure (in $mmHg$)
	· Temperature (in $°C$)	· Wind speed (in $m.s^{-1}$)
	· Humidity (in %)	· Visibility (in km)

In order to compare the performances of our proposed approach to state-of-the-art methods, the following baselines were introduced:

- **Train on Target Only (TTO):** Approach which only trains a mDNN on the target domain, without using transfer learning. The weights of the mDNN are initialised using a Glorot uniform initialisation [20].

- **Variational Autoencoder-transfer (VAE-transfer):** Approach which trains a sDNN on the source domain in an unsupervised way. The sDNN to be transferred is considered as the encoder part of a convolutional Variational Autoencoder (VAE) [177]. The encoder of a VAE learns the parameters of a Gaussian probability density characterising a compressed representation of the input in a lower dimensional space called *embedding space*. A sample is then drawn from such learned Gaussian distribution and sent as input of a decoder - DNN whose structure mirrors the encoder - which is trained to reconstruct the encoder input on its output layer. The ensemble encoder-decoder is trained to reproduce the segments of the source domain as accurately as possible. The weights of the encoder are then transferred to a mDNN. For the CogAge dataset in particular, three VAEs taking input of sizes L_{sp}, L_{sw} and L_{sg} respectively are trained and transferred.

A third approach transferring weights from the source domain without performing any fine-tuning on the target domain was also tested, but yielded performances significantly worse than all other methods. It was therefore decided not to report its result. The three aforementioned approaches are summarised in Figure 3.4.

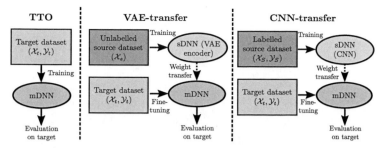

Figure 3.4: Flowchart of the three approaches tested on the CogAge dataset: TTO (no transfer), VAE-transfer and CNN-transfer. The mDNN follows the architecture described in Figure 3.5.

3.4 Experiments

In this Section, the experiments with the proposed transfer approach carried out on sensor-based HAR and ER and their results are described. The new CogAge dataset is firstly introduced, followed by the results of the experiments carried out on it. The results of the experiments obtained on *DEAP* for sensor-based ER are then presented.

3.4.1 *CogAge* dataset

Dataset description

The *CogAge* dataset was built by considering human activities as a series of simpler actions, referred to as *atomic activities*. It aggregates the data from 4 subjects performing a total of 61 different atomic activities split into two distinct categories: 6 *state activities* characterising the pose of a subject, and 55 *behavioural activities* characterising his/her behaviour. The complete list of activities is provided in Table 3.2. It can be noted that a behavioural activity can be performed while being in a particular state (e.g. drinking can be performed either while sitting or standing). Because this overlap between state and behavioural activities could potentially prevent a proper definition of classes (e.g. drinking while sitting could either be classified as drinking or sitting), two classification problems were considered, one considering exclusively the 6 state activities, the other the 55 behavioural activities.

All four subjects were asked to wear three different devices during the data acquisition process:

- **Google NEXUS 5X smartphone** placed in a subject's front left pocket, providing five different sensor modalities: three-axis accelerometer, gravity sensor, gyroscope, linear accelerometer (all sampled at $200Hz$) and magnetometer ($50Hz$).

Table 3.2: List of the state and behavioural activities of the Cognitive Village dataset. For activities with a * symbol, executions with either the left or right hand were distinguished.

State activities					
Standing	Sitting	Lying	Squatting	Walking	Bending

Behavioral activities		
Sit down	Stand up	Lie down
Get up	Squat down	Stand up from squatting
Open door*	Close door*	Open drawer*
Close drawer*	Open small box*	Close small box*
Open big box	Close big box	Open lid by rotation*
Close lid by rotation*	Open other lid*	Close other lid*
Open bag	Take from floor*	Put on floor*
Bring	Put on high position*	Take from high position*
Take out*	Eat small thing*	Drink*
Scoop and put*	Plug in*	Unplug*
Rotate*	Throw out*	Hang
Unhang	Wear jacket	Take off jacket
Read	Write*	Type*
Talk using telephone*	Touch smartphone screen*	Open tap water*
Close tap water*	Put from tap water*	Put from bottle*
Throw out water*	Gargle	Rub hands
Dry off hands by shaking	Dry off hands	Press from top*
Press by grasp*	Press switch/button*	Clean surface*
Clean floor		

- **Microsoft Band 2 smartwatch** placed on a subject's left arm, providing two different sensor modalities: three-axis accelerometer and gyroscope ($67Hz$).

- **JINS MEME glasses** placed on the subjects' head, providing five different sensor modalities: three-axis accelerometer and gyroscope ($20Hz$), blink speed, strength measurements and eye-movement measurements (all discrete signals indicating an event).

All four subjects took part in two data acquisition sessions (#1 and #2) where each of 61 atomic activities was executed at least 20 times, and each execution lasted for 5 seconds. Because the smartwatch was placed on the left arm, the choice of the arm performing some behavioural atomic actions indicated with * in Table 3.2 may impact the recognition performances. Two different datasets were therefore created for the behavioural classification problem: one gathering executions only performed by the left hand, the other gathering executions performed indifferently by the left or right hand. The former and the latter are referred to as *Behavioural Left-Hand-Only (BLHO)* and *Behavioural Both-Hands (BBH)* datasets, respectively. To build the training and testing sets, two strategies were followed: one splitting the data using a subject-dependent setup where data from the same subjects are included in the training and testing sets, the other using a subject-independent split where distinct subsets of subjects provide data for the training and testing sets. The subject-dependent classification problem has a higher simplicity, while the subject-independent one is more representative of real use-cases. For the subject-dependent split, the data from session #1 were used as a training set, those from session #2 as a testing set. The total number of executions of each dataset is summarised in Table 3.3. For the subject-independent setup, a leave-one-subject-out cross validation was performed: the data from one subject in both sessions #1 and #2 were used as testing set, and the data from the 3 other subjects as training set. All 4 subjects were used as testing subject once. The number of executions per subject is provided in Table 3.4.

Table 3.3: Number of 5-second executions for each subset of the *CogAge* dataset. Executions of session #1 and #2 were respectively used to build the training and testing sets in the subject-dependent setup.

Dataset	Session #1	Session #2
State	260	275
BLHO	1692	1705
BBH	2284	2288

Table 3.4: Number of 5-second executions for each subject of the *CogAge* dataset.

Dataset	Subject #1	Subject #2	Subject #3	Subject #4
State	165	120	120	130
BLHO	986	872	718	821
BBH	1297	1096	1078	1101

Experimental setup

Because of their different nature (data characterised by spikes instead of continuous values), the blink speed, strength and eye-movement signals of the JINS glasses were not used in this study. In addition, preliminary experiments using all devices showed that the smartphone magnetometer had little impact on the final classification performances. Our baseline study therefore used the smartphone accelerometer, gyroscope, gravity sensor, linear accelerometer, the data from the smartwatch accelerometer and gyroscope, and the data from the JINS glasses accelerometer and gyroscope.

The differences in sampling frequencies of those sensors affect the size of the 5-second segments, and the shape of the input of our DNN models. To take this into account, three different sDNNs were defined, processing data coming from the smartphone, smartwatch and smartglasses, respectively. One sDNN is associated with all channels generated from one of the three devices, as shown in Figure 3.5. The outputs of all sDNNs are then concatenated and fed into fully-connected and softmax layers, as shown in Figure 3.5.

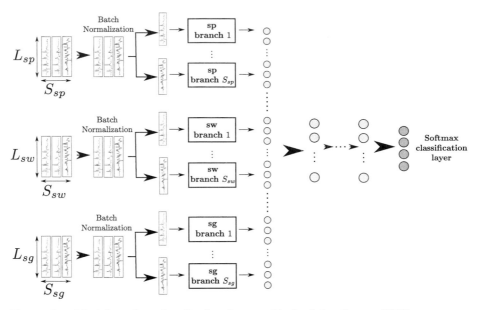

Figure 3.5: Model used on the *CogAge* dataset. Each of the three mDNNs processes the smartphone (sp), smartwatch (sw) or smartglasses (sg) data. L_* and S_* with $* \in \{sp, sw, sg\}$ refer to the segment length and number of sensor channels, respectively. Outputs from the three mDNNs are concatenated and fed into fully-connected and softmax layers.

Because of data transmission problems, all channels did not necessarily have a length of exactly 5 seconds. It was therefore decided to use the first 4 seconds of each recording. This led to segments of shape $L_{sp} \times S_{sp} = 800 \times 12$, $L_{sw} \times S_{sw} = 267 \times 6$ and $L_{sg} \times S_{sg} = 80 \times 6$ for the smartphone, smartwatch and JINS glasses, respectively. For the CNN-transfer approach, three sDNNs were trained separately for sensor modality classification on the source domain, each taking input of sizes L_{sp}, L_{sw} and L_{sg}, respectively. The resulting mDNN comprises $S = 12 + 6 + 6 = 24$ branches. The weights of each sDNN were then transferred to the mDNN of one device.

The hyper-parameters of the mDNN were firstly optimised by trial and error for TTO. Both CNN-transfer and VAE-transfer were then performed by re-using the same parameters. All DNN parameters are provided in Table 3.5. For CNN-transfer, all sDNNs were trained for 25 epochs using the ADADELTA optimiser [71] with a categorical cross-entropy loss function. For VAE-transfer, the encoder-decoder ensemble was trained for 10 epochs using an ADADELTA optimiser. A Mean Square Error reconstruction term regularised by the Kullback-Leibler divergence between the Gaussian distribution learned by the encoder and the Standard Normal Distribution was used as loss function. 90% of the source data were used as training set. The remaining 10% were used as validation set to validate the sDNN parameters. In the case of TTO, the weights of the mDNN were initialised using the Glorot uniform initialisation. The mDNN was then fine-tuned for the three classification problems - state, BLHO and BBH - using the ADADELTA optimiser with a categorical cross-entropy loss function for 150 epochs. All models were coded using the Keras [178] library (version 2.4.2) with Tensorflow backend [179] (version 1.12), and trained using a 16GB RAM machine with an Intel i7-7700K CPU and a NVidia GTX 1080Ti GPU.

Model	Parameter	Value
$sDNN_{sp}$	· # conv. + pool. + act. blocks	3
	· Conv. kernel size	(45,1), (49,1), (46,1)
	· Conv. sliding stride	(1,1), (1,1), (1,1)
	· # conv. kernels	10, 10, 10
	· Max pool. size	(2,1), (2,1), (2,1)
	· Activation	RELU
$sDNN_{sw}$	· # conv. + pool. + act. blocks	3
	· Conv. kernel size	(9,1), (11,1), (11,1)
	· Conv. sliding stride	(1,1), (1,1), (1,1)
	· # conv. kernels	10, 10, 10
	· Max pool. size	(2,1), (2,1), (2,1)
	· Activation	RELU
$sDNN_{sg}$	· # conv. + pool. + act. blocks	3
	· Conv. kernel size	(5,1), (5,1), (5,1)
	· Conv. sliding stride	(1,1), (1,1), (1,1)
	· # conv. kernels	10, 10, 10
	· Max pool. size	(2,1), (2,1), (2,1)
	· Activation	RELU
$mDNN$	· # dense layers	3
	· # neurons per layer	2000, 2000, 2000
	· Activation	RELU

Table 3.5: Hyper-parameters of the sDNNs and mDNN used on the *CogAge* dataset. The parameter values are given assuming that the input of the models is of size $T \times S$ where T is the length of the multichannel segments along the time axis and S the number of sensor channels. *sp*, *sw* and *sg* stand for smartphone, smartwatch and smartglasses, respectively. The same architectures were used for TTO, CNN-transfer and VAE-transfer. For VAE-transfer, the reported sDNNs were used as encoders of a VAE trained on the source dataset.

The accuracy, the average F1-score (AF1) and Mean Average Precision (MAP) were used as evaluation metrics. The MAP is based on the computation of class Average Precisions (APs). For each class, test examples are ordered by decreasing probabilities provided by the softmax layer of a mDNN. Precisions are then computed at each position of an example of the class in the ordered list. Those precisions are then averaged to compute the AP of the class, and the class APs averaged to yield the MAP. Because of potential overlapping between state and behavioural activities, AP is a convenient metric for examining whether an execution was preferentially classified into the most relevant class or not.

Results and discussion

The results of the three classification problems are provided in Table 3.6 for the subject-dependent configuration and Table 3.7 for the subject-independent one. The main observations for both setups can be highlighted as follows:

- The results of the state classification problem are relatively uniform across the transfer and the baseline approaches. This can be attributed to two factors. Firstly, the state classification problem is significantly simpler than BBH or BLHO because it contains a low number of fairly distinct classes. Secondly, the fairly small size of the testing set which makes a few misclassified examples result in a drop of a few percent in evaluation metrics. With these factors in mind, it can be observed that CNN-transfer, TTO and VAE-transfer all return predictions on the testing set differ only on a few examples.

- For behavioural activity classification, VAE-transfer performs mediocre overall, and ends up yielding results worse than both CNN-transfer and TTO.

- Our transfer approach consistently yields better results than TTO for both BLHO and BBH classification problems. It can be noted that CNN-transfer provides better performances than TTO for all test subjects in the subject-independent configuration.

Table 3.6: Accuracies, Average F1-Scores and MAPs (in %) obtained by TTO, VAE-transfer and CNN-transfer for the state, BLHO and BBH classification problems in the subject-dependent configuration.

Transfer approach	State			BLHO			BBH		
	Acc.	AF1	MAP	Acc.	AF1	MAP	Acc.	AF1	MAP
TTO	95.91	**95.94**	97.63	71.95	71.72	75.03	67.94	67.65	72.00
VAE-transfer	94.78	94.77	**97.93**	64.44	64.09	67.37	61.31	61.04	65.18
CNN-transfer	**95.94**	**95.94**	97.62	**76.44**	**76.07**	**79.09**	**71.85**	**71.41**	**75.14**

A detailed analysis of class APs for behavioural activities was carried out in the subject-dependent configuration to examine whether some transfer setups could be beneficial to particular activities or not. Figures 3.6, 3.7 and 3.8 show the different class AP obtained for State, BLHO and BBH classification, respectively.

While differences between the three tested approaches were small for state classification, the superiority of CNN-transfer for the classification of behavioural activities could be observed by computing some global statistics on all activities.

Table 3.7: Accuracies, Average F1-Scores and MAPs (in %) obtained by TTO, VAE-transfer and CNN-transfer for the state, BLHO and BBH classification problems in the subject-independent configuration (leave-one-subject-out cross-validation).

Transfer approach	Fold index	State			BLHO			BBH		
		Acc.	AF1	MAP	Acc.	AF1	MAP	Acc.	AF1	MAP
TTO	1	87.27	86.95	93.73	33.81	32.23	31.87	29.77	26.52	29.96
	2	91.67	91.57	95.19	52.47	50.37	52.32	46.45	44.01	46.24
	3	95.99	94.16	95.99	34.61	30.51	33.55	30.58	28.74	32.93
	4	90.66	90.82	97.15	55.52	52.01	56.96	47.69	44.27	47.71
	Average	**91.40**	**90.88**	**95.52**	44.10	41.28	43.68	38.62	35.89	39.21
	Standard-deviation	3.59	2.98	1.44	11.50	11.48	12.82	9.77	9.58	9.07
VAE-transfer	1	83.58	83.13	88.13	35.02	31.62	30.35	31.74	28.61	28.02
	2	90.00	89.66	93.26	51.58	47.99	52.65	43.48	42.09	43.89
	3	95.00	94.95	98.59	35.18	32.06	36.84	29.01	28.54	31.51
	4	82.58	76.35	93.79	54.43	50.03	52.54	48.23	43.61	46.38
	Average	87.79	86.02	93.45	44.05	40.43	43.10	38.12	35.71	37.45
	Standard-deviation	5.82	8.06	4.28	10.40	9.95	11.29	9.21	8.27	9.04
CNN-transfer	1	88.21	87.56	92.40	36.33	33.99	35.39	33.57	30.05	31.07
	2	84.17	83.89	92.58	52.98	49.34	53.92	47.23	45.33	51.15
	3	98.33	98.33	98.01	38.28	33.66	40.66	32.94	32.52	36.03
	4	91.52	91.56	96.60	58.85	55.40	62.04	50.19	46.60	53.86
	Average	90.56	90.34	94.90	**49.39**	**43.10**	**48.00**	**40.98**	**38.63**	**43.03**
	Standard-deviation	5.99	6.18	2.84	11.68	10.99	12.18	9.01	8.55	11.18

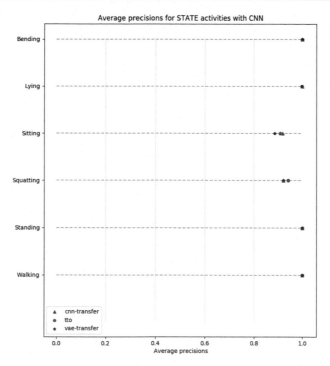

Figure 3.6: Average precisions for the six state activities of the *CogAge* dataset obtained by TTO, CNN-transfer and VAE-transfer.

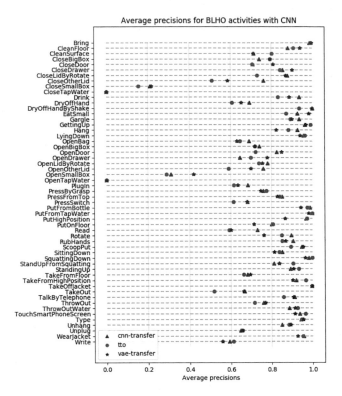

Figure 3.7: Average precisions for the 55 behavioural activities of the *CogAge* dataset in the BLHO configuration obtained by TTO, CNN-transfer and VAE-transfer.

CNN-transfer yielded better class APs than TTO for 35/55 and 41/55 behavioural activities for BLHO and BBH, respectively. For the activities for which it provided the best APs, CNN-transfer obtained a 5.76% and 6.02% average improvement compared to TTO for the BLHO and BBH classification, respectively. For others activities, CNN-transfer underperformed TTO by smaller margins, with an average AP gap of 3.11% and 3.37% for the BLHO and BBH classification, respectively. The overall results suggest that CNN-transfer obtains notable performance improvements over TTO for the recognition of some activities, while still keeping reasonable performances for activities where TTO outperforms it. It is, however, difficult to identify specific activities which benefit more from transfer than the others. It could in particular be checked that *CogAge* activities such as open/close doors/drawers which are quite common in the OPPORTUNITY source dataset (as shown in Table 2.1) did not always have better recognition performances after transfer.

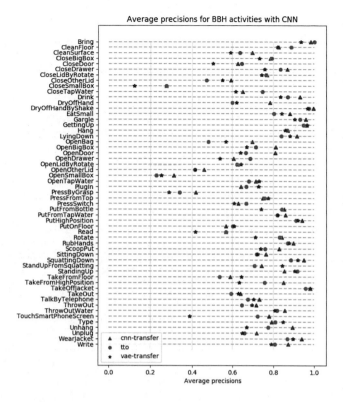

Figure 3.8: Average precisions for the 55 behavioural activities of the *CogAge* dataset in the BBH configuration obtained by TTO, CNN-transfer and VAE-transfer.

3.4.2 *DEAP* dataset

Dataset description

The *DEAP* dataset aggregates data from 32 subjects who watched 40 one-minute-long music videos, selected to induce a wide range of emotions. During the experiments, each subject was wearing on their head a sensor equipment yielding a total of 40 sensor channels ($S = 40$): 32 EEG channels and 8 channels returning peripheral physiological signals (EOG, EMG, GSR, BVP, temperature and respiration). The labelling was performed using the Circumplex model which decomposes emotions along two main axes: arousal (level of excitement) and valence (level of pleasantness). Each subject was asked after each visualisation to rate their level of arousal and valence on a 9-point scale from 1 (very low) to 9 (very high). The pre-processed version of the dataset was used, with all 40 channels downsampled to a frequency of $128Hz$.

Experimental setup

To evaluate data labelled using the Circumplex model, numerous studies defined emotion recognition either as a two-class problem between low ($<$ 5) and high ($\geqslant$ 5) arousal/valence, or three-class problem between low ($<$ 3), medium ($\geqslant$ 3 and $<$ 6) and high ($\geqslant$ 6). Sensor-based ER is still a relatively immature research topic due to its inherent difficulty caused by several factors such as challenges to obtain properly labelled data, the high intra-class variability when using physiological signals, etc. As a result, a large part of the ER literature performed experiments in a subject-dependent context, while the few subject-independent studies could only report mediocre classification results [180, 181]. It was therefore decided to use the subject-dependent setup of [157] in which the authors trained a bi-modal autoencoder processing both EEG and other modalities and taking non-overlapping segments of 1 second ($L = 128$) as inputs for a two-class classification problem for arousal and valence. The data segments from all 32 subjects of the *DEAP* dataset were mixed and evenly split into folds for a 10-fold cross-validation. In the following experiments, two mDNNs with $S = 40$ branches were trained, one for arousal and the other for valence classification. Both are evaluated using the classification accuracy as evaluation metric.

Similarly to the *CogAge* dataset, the parameters of the mDNN were firstly optimised for TTO by trial and error, and then re-used for CNN-transfer. For VAE-transfer however, better performances could be obtained by changing the neural activation function of the sDNNs. All DNN parameters are provided in Table 3.8. For CNN-transfer and each of arousal and valence classifications, a sDNN was trained for 100 epochs using the ADADELTA optimiser with a categorical cross-entropy loss function. For VAE-transfer, the same training setup as described in Section 3.4.1 for the *CogAge* dataset is used. 90% of the source data were used as training set. The remaining 10% were used as validation set to validate the sDNN parameters. Weights of the sDNN were transferred to construct a mDNN on the target domain. The rest of the weights of the mDNN were initialised using the Glorot uniform initialisation [20]. Two mDNNs - one for arousal and the other for valence - were then fine-tuned for each fold using the ADADELTA optimiser with a categorical cross-entropy loss function for 300 epochs.

Results and discussion

The results for arousal and valence classification on the *DEAP* dataset are summarised in Tables 3.9 and 3.10, respectively. Similarly to the *CogAge* dataset, VAE-transfer was again outperformed by both CNN-transfer and TTO. CNN-transfer consistently outperformed TTO on all 10 folds for both arousal and valence classification problems. This validates the effectiveness of our transfer approach. In addition, our method yielded significantly better results than those obtained in [157] using bi-modal AEs.

Model	Parameter	Value
sDNN (CNN-transfer)	· # conv. + pool. + act. blocks	3
	· Conv. kernel size	(9,1), (9,1), (9,1)
	· Conv. sliding stride	(1,1), (1,1), (1,1)
	· # conv. kernels	10, 10, 10
	· Max pool. size	(2,1), (2,1), (2,1)
	· Activation	RELU
sDNN (VAE-transfer)	· # conv. + pool. + act. blocks	3
	· Conv. kernel size	(9,1), (9,1), (9,1)
	· Conv. sliding stride	(1,1), (1,1), (1,1)
	· # conv. kernels	10, 10, 10
	· Max pool. size	(2,1), (2,1), (2,1)
	· Activation	tanh
$mDNN$	· # dense layers	3
	· # neurons per layer	1000, 500, 100
	· Activation	RELU

Table 3.8: Hyper-parameters of the sDNN and mDNN used on the *DEAP* dataset. The parameter values are given assuming that the input of the models is of size $T \times S$ where T is the length of the multichannel segments along the time axis and S the number of sensor channels. For VAE-transfer, the reported sDNN was used as encoder of a VAE trained on the source dataset.

Table 3.9: 10-fold cross validation accuracies (in %) for the classification of AROUSAL using a multichannel DNN on the *DEAP* dataset. F_i refers to fold number i.

Approach	F1	F2	F3	F4	F5	F6	F7	F8	F9	F10	Average
Bi-modal AE [157]	-	-	-	-	-	-	-	-	-	-	80.50
TTO	89.26	88.13	87.55	87.69	88.13	88.05	88.64	88.75	87.59	87.91	88.17
VAE-transfer	83.22	84.87	84.93	85.04	83.74	84.86	84.71	84.55	85.12	83.93	84.50
CNN-transfer	90.89	91.60	91.18	91.46	91.37	91.53	90.79	91.59	91.64	90.80	91.29

Table 3.10: 10-fold cross validation accuracies (in %) for the classification of VA-LENCE using a multichannel DNN on the *DEAP* dataset. F_i refers to fold number i.

Approach	F1	F2	F3	F4	F5	F6	F7	F8	F9	F10	Average
Bi-modal AE [157]	-	-	-	-	-	-	-	-	-	-	85.20
TTO	87.67	87.03	87.85	86.93	87.26	87.44	88.03	87.08	87.75	87.25	87.43
VAE-transfer	85.17	84.86	83.92	85.48	84.75	84.06	84.23	85.42	84.90	84.69	84.75
CNN-transfer	90.89	91.12	90.22	90.39	90.51	90.27	90.71	90.39	91.08	90.84	90.64

3.4.3 Analysis of transfer robustness to variations in training data quantity

The experiments on both *CogAge* and *DEAP* datasets showed that the best performances were obtained by our transfer method based on supervised pre-training using sensor modality labels. Our transfer approach is based on the assumption that it could help in cases where labelled training data on the target dataset are scarce. In order to further check this assumption, additional experiments with reduced amounts of training data on both *CogAge* (subject-dependent configuration) and *DEAP* datasets were carried out. On both target datasets, the training dataset was randomly downsampled to 5, 25, 50 and 75% of its original size while keeping the same number of testing examples, and compute the classification performances on the same number of testing examples. Tables 3.11, 3.12 and 3.13 show the results for State/BLHO/BBH classification on *CogAge*, arousal classification on *DEAP*, and valence classification on *DEAP*, respectively.

Table 3.11: Accuracies, AF1s and MAPs (in %) of TTO, VAE-transfer and CNN-transfer after downsampling of the training set, for the classification of state, BLHO and BBH activities on the *CogAge* dataset (subject-dependent configuration).

Transfer approach	Training target data proportion (%)	State			BLHO			BBH		
		Acc.	AF1	MAP	Acc.	AF1	MAP	Acc.	AF1	MAP
TTO	5	66.56	61.51	68.70	19.05	16.24	16.62	19.86	15.31	15.82
	25	88.78	88.92	94.16	51.98	51.23	50.90	50.83	50.21	52.67
	50	93.78	93.67	96.88	60.89	60.74	62.07	58.90	58.39	61.99
	75	95.14	95.18	97.73	71.11	71.24	73.18	62.78	62.70	65.99
	100	95.91	95.94	97.63	71.95	71.72	75.03	67.94	67.65	72.00
VAE transfer	5	59.79	57.44	64.55	19.05	14.88	17.43	15.11	13.03	13.49
	25	89.14	88.92	91.42	39.20	37.34	38.53	32.92	32.46	33.00
	50	89.09	89.05	95.69	51.91	51.52	52.79	47.52	47.36	49.18
	75	94.84	94.81	97.91	61.45	60.58	62.35	51.29	50.60	53.90
	100	94.78	94.77	97.93	64.44	64.09	67.37	61.31	61.04	65.18
CNN transfer	5	67.64	67.70	73.74	23.39	18.10	20.41	25.92	22.05	24.13
	25	90.47	90.61	94.12	55.89	55.46	56.97	56.95	55.65	57.51
	50	94.60	94.47	97.73	66.66	66.01	68.59	62.83	62.22	66.22
	75	95.88	95.87	97.11	73.06	72.47	74.99	66.29	66.29	69.95
	100	95.94	95.94	97.62	76.44	76.07	79.09	71.85	71.41	75.14

The main observation is that CNN-transfer keeps outperforming TTO at all levels of downsampling of the target training sets. CNN-transfer yields a consistent improvement for both BLHO and BBH problems compared to TTO at all downsampling levels. Performances on the state classification remain relatively uniform between all three tested methods in most configurations due to the highest simplicity of the problem. Larger differences in performances can be observed in the case where the training set was downsampled the most (5%). In this configuration, CNN-transfer clearly outperforms the two other approaches which indicates its effectiveness in configurations with few training examples. The same consistency can be observed on the *DEAP* dataset as CNN-transfer also outperformed TTO on all 10 folds of the dataset. VAE-transfer remains outperformed by both TTO and CNN-transfer in most tested configurations.

Table 3.12: 10-fold cross validation accuracies (in %) of TTO, VAE-transfer and CNN-transfer after downsampling of the training set for the classification of AROUSAL on the *DEAP* dataset. F_i refers to fold number i.

Transfer approach	Training target data proportion (%)	F1	F2	F3	F4	F5	F6	F7	F8	F9	F10	Average
TTO	5	64.11	64.81	64.00	63.64	63.81	65.49	65.74	67.44	64.62	64.61	64.83
	25	78.47	76.28	76.08	76.66	76.75	77.53	74.91	76.92	77.80	76.23	76.76
	50	82.08	81.56	82.29	84.34	82.03	83.94	82.68	82.42	82.90	83.16	82.74
	75	85.88	87.49	87.25	85.16	87.05	85.13	85.59	86.22	86.86	85.88	86.25
	100	89.26	88.13	87.55	87.69	88.13	88.05	88.64	88.75	87.59	87.91	88.17
VAE transfer	5	63.52	64.26	64.20	65.80	64.83	64.24	64.42	64.91	64.04	63.70	63.70
	25	74.12	74.79	74.59	74.78	74.45	74.63	73.76	74.49	74.09	73.67	74.34
	50	78.99	79.92	80.31	80.05	79.50	80.25	79.49	79.34	79.77	79.12	79.67
	75	82.14	83.07	82.56	83.12	82.54	82.13	82.48	82.69	82.19	82.25	82.52
	100	83.22	84.87	84.93	85.04	83.74	84.86	84.71	84.55	85.12	83.93	84.50
CNN transfer	5	65.66	65.58	65.91	66.64	65.71	65.45	66.94	65.31	66.90	66.48	66.06
	25	79.86	80.47	79.97	80.34	79.59	78.91	79.58	80.05	80.39	80.18	79.93
	50	86.79	86.95	86.32	86.77	86.48	87.54	86.41	86.58	86.78	86.76	86.74
	75	89.37	89.66	89.46	90.60	89.72	89.74	89.12	89.55	89.66	88.81	89.57
	100	90.89	91.60	91.18	91.46	91.37	91.53	90.79	91.59	91.64	90.80	91.29

Table 3.13: 10-fold cross validation accuracies (in %) of TTO, VAE-transfer and CNN-transfer after downsampling of the training set for the classification of VALENCE on the *DEAP* dataset. F_i refers to fold number i.

Transfer approach	Training target data proportion (%)	F1	F2	F3	F4	F5	F6	F7	F8	F9	F10	Average
TTO	5	64.27	64.36	64.29	62.71	63.86	63.50	63.08	65.17	63.76	62.79	63.78
	25	77.78	75.60	76.33	76.23	76.26	74.88	75.93	76.12	76.44	76.07	76.16
	50	82.49	81.78	81.89	81.88	81.63	82.61	81.36	81.87	82.76	83.21	82.15
	75	85.42	85.97	84.76	85.64	85.21	85.62	84.92	86.21	85.13	86.04	85.49
	100	87.67	87.03	87.85	86.93	87.26	87.44	88.03	87.08	87.75	87.25	87.43
VAE transfer	5	64.11	64.43	63.29	65.05	64.55	65.22	64.14	65.35	64.72	65.38	64.62
	25	74.67	73.57	74.31	74.70	73.26	74.32	74.52	74.02	74.48	74.18	74.20
	50	80.41	80.11	79.94	80.49	80.13	80.11	80.12	80.12	80.53	79.33	80.22
	75	83.79	82.68	82.73	83.95	83.33	82.68	82.78	82.85	83.41	82.96	83.12
	100	85.17	84.86	83.92	85.48	84.75	84.06	84.23	85.42	84.90	82.96	83.12
CNN transfer	5	65.31	64.94	65.48	64.16	63.96	64.19	65.45	65.25	65.43	65.15	64.93
	25	80.27	79.91	78.81	79.01	79.50	80.01	79.32	81.47	79.45	80.38	79.81
	50	86.44	86.37	85.60	86.77	85.16	85.71	85.54	85.68	86.74	86.71	86.07
	75	88.86	89.43	89.09	88.98	89.35	88.75	89.01	89.53	88.85	89.45	89.13
	100	90.89	91.12	90.22	90.39	90.51	90.27	90.71	90.39	91.08	90.84	90.64

3.4.4 Analysis of transfer interpretability

To gain better understanding of the performance improvements of our transfer approach compared to the approach without transfer, a low-level analysis on neurons of a mDNN was performed to identify differences between TTO and CNN-transfer. On both *CogAge* (subject-dependent setup) and *DEAP*, TTO and CNN-transfer were respectively used to train two mDNNs with the same architecture (shown in Figure 3.5). For each neuron or layer of this architecture, one can compare metrics computed on the mDNN trained with TTO to those on the mDNN trained with CNN-transfer. This way, one can find out in which neurons and layers the biggest differences (or similarities) can be found between TTO and CNN-transfer.

115

Given two trained mDNNs - one using TTO and the other using CNN-transfer - an importance score was computed for each neuron that indicates its relevance (and the one of the feature it encodes) to the target classification problem. For this, the *Neuron Importance Score Propagation (NISP)* [182] and *Infinite Feature Selection (InfFS)* [183] methods were used. NISP can be applied to any DNN involving fully-connected, convolutional or pooling layers. It is a score backpropagation method which assumes that importance scores are available for the neurons on the penultimate layer (i.e. last one before the softmax layer). Those scores can be obtained by any feature ranking approach. Similarly to [182], the InfFS method was chosen to compute them, mainly since it showed its effectiveness for DNN architectures involving convolutional layers. NISP then backpropagates the InfFS scores to the prior layers so that an importance score can be attributed to each neuron of the DNN. Let $n^{(k)}$ be the number of neurons of the kth layer, $s_i^{(k)}$ be the importance score of the ith neuron of the kth layer ($1 \leqslant k \leqslant n^{(k)}$), $w_{ij}^{(k)}$ be the weight connecting the ith neuron of the $(k-1)^{th}$ layer to the jth neuron of the kth layer ($1 \leqslant i \leqslant n^{(k-1)}$ and $1 \leqslant j \leqslant n^{(k)}$). Then $s_i^{(k)}$ is computed as[2]

$$s_i^{(k)} = \sum_{j=1}^{n^{(k+1)}} |w_{ij}^{(k)}| s_j^{(k+1)} \qquad (3.3)$$

In other words, the importance score of a neuron in a layer is the sum of the scores of all neurons of the next layer that it has a connection with, weighted by the absolute value of the neural weights.

The study was carried out for both BBH and BLHO classification on the *CogAge* dataset, following the hypothesis that the largest performance gap between TTO and CNN-transfer would lead to the clearest differences between their neuron importance scores. Using NISP and InfFS, vectors of neuron importance scores were obtained for all layers of both mDNNs trained using TTO and CNN-transfer. The vectors of importance scores of the kth layer are referred to as $v_{TTO}^{(k)} = \{s_{1,TTO}^{(k)}, \ldots, s_{n^{(k)},TTO}^{(k)}\} \in \mathbb{R}^{n^{(k)}}$ and $v_{CT}^{(k)} = \{s_{1,CT}^{(k)}, \ldots, s_{n^{(k)},CT}^{(k)}\} \in \mathbb{R}^{n^{(k)}}$ for TTO and CNN-transfer, respectively. A min-max normalisation on each $v_*^{(k)} \in \mathbb{R}^{n^{(k)}}$ (with $* \in \{TTO, CT\}$) was then applied to obtain a normalised vector of scores $\widetilde{v}_*^{(k)} \in \mathbb{R}^{n^{(k)}}$. Because NISP backpropagates only positive scores, the absolute values of neuron importance scores in one layer increase as the layer is closer to the input of the DNN. This normalisation was performed to allow comparison between scores of layers independently of their depth. For all layers, the Euclidean distance between both $\widetilde{v}_{TTO}^{(k)}$ and $\widetilde{v}_{CT}^{(k)}$ were finally computed by

$$D^{(k)} = ||\widetilde{v}_{TTO}^{(k)} - \widetilde{v}_{CT}^{(k)}||_2 \qquad (3.4)$$

---

[2]This formula can be used to backpropagate importance scores in fully-connected layers. How to apply it to convolutional and pooling layers can be found in the supplementary materials of [182].

that is referred to as the *difference of the kth layer*. This allows to determine which layers were the most similar or dissimilar after the training using TTO and CNN-transfer. Figures 3.10 and 3.9 respectively show the layer differences $D^{(k)}$ arranged in decreasing order for BLHO and BBH.

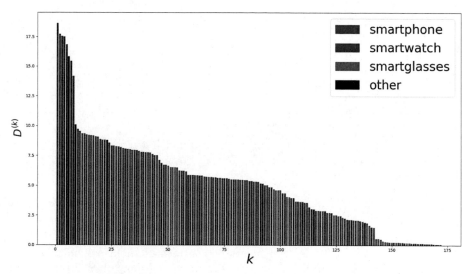

Figure 3.9: Layer differences $D^{(k)}$ for all layers of mDNNs trained using TTO and CNN-transfer for BBH classification on the *CogAge* dataset. Each bar corresponds to a layer and represents its difference between TTO and CNN-transfer. Layer differences are arranged in decreasing order. For each of them, we indicate if it was computed for a layer belonging to a branch processing smartphone, smartwatch or smartglasses data. Layers not belonging to any branch (e.g. concatenation or fully-connected layers) are categorised as "other".

As shown in Figures 3.10 and 3.9, the differences in neuron importance scores between TTO and CNN-transfer are fairly significant for some layers. Since each layer encodes specific features, this indicates differences in the features learned using either CNN-transfer or TTO. The features encoded by the layers with the highest score differences between TTO and CNN-transfer were analysed more closely. As shown in Figure 3.5, each layer belonging to one branch processes data coming from a certain device, i.e. smartphone, smartwatch or smartglasses. Layers were thereofre categorised depending on the device (as depicted by the colours in Figures 3.10 and 3.9). Layers not belonging to any branch (e.g. concatenation or fully-connected layers) were categorised as "other". It could be observed that layers with the highest differences encode features computed on data coming from the smartwatch and smarthphone.

Preliminary experiments using each device individually for behavioural activity classification showed that the smartwatch was the most important device, followed by the smartphone. This indicates that those devices also provide the most relevant

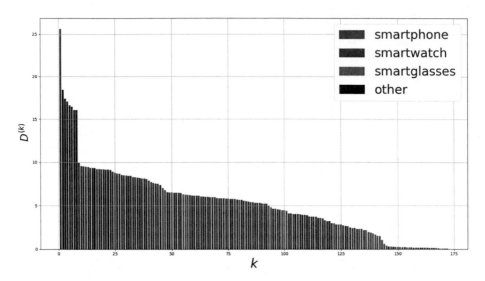

Figure 3.10: Layer differences $D^{(k)}$ for all layers of mDNNs trained using TTO and CNN-transfer for BLHO classification on the *CogAge* dataset. Each bar corresponds to a layer and represents its difference between TTO and CNN-transfer. Layer differences are arranged in decreasing order. For each of them, we indicate if it was computed for a layer belonging to a branch processing smartphone, smartwatch or smartglasses data. Layers not belonging to any branch (e.g. concatenation or fully-connected layers) are categorised as "other".

features. This could be confirmed by checking which channels of the input data were the most important to the classification of behavioural activities. For this, the *Jacobian matrices* of the mDNN trained by TTO or CNN-transfer were computed, following an approach similar to [184]. The mDNN estimates the predictive function $f_T : \mathbb{R}^{L \times S} \to \mathbb{R}^{C_T}$, where L is the length of a multichannel segment X belonging to the target dataset $\mathcal{X}_T$, S is the number of channels of this segment, and C_T is the number of classes. The multichannel segment $X = (x_{ls})_{l,s} \in \mathbb{R}^{L \times S}$ is a $L \times S$ matrix where each element x_{ls} represents the value at the lth time point $(1 \leq l \leq L)$ of the sth sensor channel $(1 \leq s \leq S)$. In addition, f_T associates X to a vector of softmax probabilities for C_T classes, $f_T(X) = (f_{T,1}(X), \cdots, f_{T,c}(X), \cdots, f_{T,C_T}(X))$ $(1 \leq c \leq C_T)$. Under this setting, a *Jacobian value* is defined as

$$J_{c,l,s}(X) = \frac{\partial}{\partial x_{ls}} f_{T,c}(X) \tag{3.5}$$

This provides the information on how much the variation in x_{ls} affects the softmax probability for the cth class. $J_{c,l,s}(X)$ can be used to determine which x_{ls} in X would matter the most for the classification of X into the cth class: the smaller $J_{c,l,s}(X)$ is (in absolute value), the less impact variations in x_{ls} are, and therefore the less important x_{ls} is. In contrast, x_{ls} associated to higher $J_{c,l,s}(X)$ (in absolute value) are more important.

This reasoning was applied "channel-wise" to X. In particular, a *channel-wise Jacobian score for X $\omega_s(X)$* was computed as the average of absolute $J_{c,l,s}(X)$ over all the L time points and all the C_T classes, that is

$$\omega_s(X) = \frac{1}{C_T} \frac{1}{L} \sum_{c=1}^{C_T} \sum_{l=1}^{L} |J_{c,l,s}(X)| \tag{3.6}$$

$\omega_s(X)$ indicates the overall importance of the sth channel for the classification of X. Finally, a *global channel-wise Jacobian score* Ω_s was computed by averaging $\omega_s(X)$ over all segments in $\mathcal{X}_T$:

$$\Omega_s = \frac{1}{card(\mathcal{X}_T)} \sum_{X \in \mathcal{X}_T} \omega_s(X) \tag{3.7}$$

A high value of Ω_s indicates a high importance of the sth sensor channel for the classification problem.

Figures 3.11 and 3.12 show the values of Ω_s obtained for both mDNNs trained by TTO and CNN-transfer for the $S = 24$ sensor channels for BBH and BLHO classification on the *CogAge* dataset, respectively. It can be observed that the scores obtained for both CNN-transfer and TTO do not significantly differ. For both of them, some input sensor channels such as smartphone gyroscope ($k \in \{7, 8, 9\}$ in Figure 3.11) and linear acceleration ($k \in \{10, 11, 12\}$), all smartwatch modalities ($k \in \{13, 14, 15, 16, 17, 18\}$) contribute more to the target task than the others, especially accelerometer and gyroscope of the smartglasses ($k \in \{19, 20, 21, 22, 23, 24\}$). The highest Jacobian scores are obtained for channels of the smartwatch, which matches the observations on our preliminary experiments on the *CogAge* dataset.

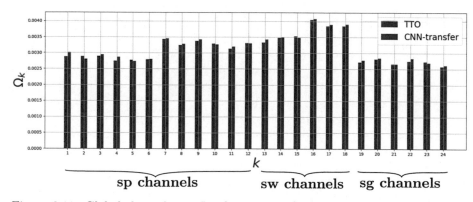

Figure 3.11: Global channel-wise Jacobian scores Ω_k for mDNNs trained by TTO (red) and CNN-transfer (blue). These scores are computed for BBH on the testing set of the *CogAge* dataset. Data channels 1 to 12, 13 to 18 and 19 to 24 are provided by the smartphone, smartwatch and smartglasses, respectively.

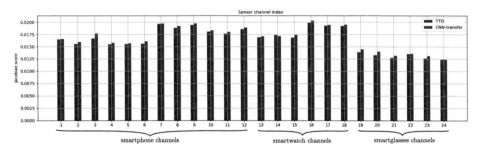

Figure 3.12: Global channel-wise Jacobian scores Ω_k for mDNNs trained by TTO (red) and CNN-transfer (blue). These scores are computed for BLHO on the testing set of the *CogAge* dataset. Data channels 1 to 12, 13 to 18 and 19 to 24 are provided by the smartphone, smartwatch and smartglasses, respectively.

The NISP+InfFS and Jacobian experiments for behavioral activity classification on the *CogAge* dataset showed that the layers of the mDNN processing the most useful sensor channels (as shown in both Figures 3.12 and 3.11) also had the largest differences in importance scores between TTO and CNN-transfer (fig:layer-scores). The largest score differences were found in layers processing smartwatch data, which is the device providing the most important data for BBH and BLHO classification for both TTO and CNN-transfer. This indicates that the transferred features on the most important channels were successfully fine-tuned into more discriminative features, while not causing loss of information in the other channels. Our future work will focus on confirming whether this phenomenon also occurs for different target domains by carrying out the same experiments on other target datasets.

3.5 Summary

In this Section, a deep transfer learning approach - referred to as CNN-transfer - was proposed that could generally be applied to a variety of classification problems using non-sparse time-series data. It is based on the idea to use sensor modality classification as a proxy source task to learn transferable general time-series features. A source dataset containing as many different sensor modalities as possible is firstly built by aggregating existing time-series datasets used for various applications. The data records in the source dataset are then segmented, labelled with their corresponding sensor modality and used to train a sDNN. On the target domain, a mDNN is constructed by replicating and fine-tuning the sDNN for each of the sensor channels of the target dataset. The architecture of the mDNN allows to handle different target domains regardless of their numbers of sensor channels. This approach was tested against two baselines - TTO and VAE-transfer - on two very different target domains: wearable-based HAR and ER.

For both applications, the proposed transfer method led to better classification performances than the two baselines, which indicates that it is robust to variations in type and format of the target data. It is also robust to variations in quantity of the training data on the target domain, since CNN-transfer outperformed TTO for different amounts of training data on both the *CogAge* and *DEAP* datasets. It is believed that this method could let researchers bypass the issue of target data scarcity by leveraging existing time-series datasets. This assumption is comforted by the fact that the *CogAge* and *DEAP* experiments showed that information relevant to the target problem could in particular be extracted from completely unrelated source datasets, in accordance with previous findings in the literature [46, 158]. Although further experiments would be needed to confirm whether such results can be reproduced on other target domains, it is possible to foresee that the proposed CNN-transfer approach could be useful for ubiquitous computing applications, where acquiring large quantities of labelled data for a specific problem is difficult, but a high number of datasets for various applications is available.

Despite the extensive experiments presented in this Section, the following two points require further investigation. The first one concerns the limited scope of the studies which were carried out. It could be expanded by analysing the impact of adding, removing or picking specific sensor modalities and datasets from the source domain, which could give a better assessment of the robustness of the proposed method. Following an approach similar to [46], the influence of the amount of source data, number and granularity of the classes on the source domain could be checked more in detail in future studies. Additionally, adding different types of time-series in the source domain (e.g. sparse time-series, event-based data, etc.) could be useful to check whether CNN-transfer can also be applied to target applications not using non-sparse time-series data. Finally, testing its performances on additional target domains could verify its generality on a larger scale.

The second point is to provide a further interpretation of the features transferred from the source to the target domain, and why they allow classification models to perform better than not using transfer on the target domain. Some initial insights have been provided in this Section by computing neuron importance scores (relatively to the target classification) using the NISP and InfFS approaches, and the mDNN Jacobian matrix on the *CogAge* dataset. Those experiments showed that CNN-transfer obtains different and more relevant features than the ones obtained by TTO, by re-adapting the transferred features during the fine-tuning phase. However, such analysis remained on a general level by comparing mDNNs trained by CNN-transfer and TTO in a layer-wise fashion. Future works could focus on checking how importance scores differ for each layer. In particular, importance scores and their distribution among the neurons of each layer could be analysed to identify which of the features learned on the source domain were the most useful for the target domain.

3.6 Complementary experiments

In order to further test the generalisation capacities of the proposed transfer method, additional experiments were carried out on the sensor-based ER dataset ELISE, and the sensor-based PR dataset PainMonit respectively introduced in Sections 1.2.2 and 1.2.3.

3.6.1 *ELISE* - transfer for sensor-based emotion recognition

The proposed CNN-transfer with the same source domain as the one used in the experiments of Section 3 was applied to the ELISE dataset (presented in Section 1.2.2 and [53]) for the classification of four emotional states (happiness, frustration, boredom, other) using EEG, BVP, PPG, EOG, GSR and temperature data. Following the experimental setup described in [53], the study was carried out in a subject-dependent and subject-independent setup. The performances of CNN-transfer are reported against those of three baselines: one using feature engineering (HCF) as reported in [53] and Table 1.2, another using feature learning with a regular CNN architecture with 2D convolutional layers, and the last one using the same multichannel architecture as CNN-transfer but without transfer (mCNN TTO). The hyper-parameters of all DNN-models were manually fine-tuned and are reported in Table 3.15. The same approach as the one reported in Section 3.4 was followed for multichannel architectures: the mDNN hyper-parameters were firstly optimised for TTO, and then re-used to perform CNN-transfer. The classification performances of all approaches are reported in Table 3.14.

AF1 (%)	Subject-dependent	Subject-independent
HCF [53]	91.49	28.85
CNN	34.95	15.99
mCNN TTO	41.69	26.73
mCNN CNN-transfer	49.16	29.78

Table 3.14: Average F1-scores for the classification of happiness, frustration, boredom and other on the ELISE dataset. For the subject-dependent case, the AF1 averaged over all 5 folds is reported.

The main observations from the results shown in Table 3.14 are as follows:

- Deep-learning-based feature extraction approaches still struggle to yield satisfying results on the ELISE dataset in the subject-dependent configurations.

- mCNN with CNN-transfer performs the best in the subject-independent configuration.

- the mCNN architecture outperforms the regular 2D CNN architecture commonly used to process multichannel time-series data frames.

122

Model	Parameter	Value
CNN	· # conv. + pool. + act. blocks	3
	· Conv. kernel size	(41,1), (21,1), (11,1)
	· Conv. sliding stride	(1,1), (1,1), (1,1)
	· # conv. kernels	10, 10, 10
	· Max pool. size	(2,1), (2,1), (2,1)
	· Activation	RELU
	· Dense layers	2
	· # neurons per layer	1000, 100
sDNN	· # conv. + pool. + act. blocks	3
(for both TTO	· Conv. kernel size	(41,1), (21,1), (11,1)
and CNN-transfer)	· Conv. sliding stride	(1,1), (1,1), (1,1)
	· # conv. kernels	10, 10, 10
	· Max pool. size	(2,1), (2,1), (2,1)
	· Activation	RELU
mDNN	· # dense layers	2
(for both TTO and	· # neurons per layer	1000, 100
CNN-transfer)	· Activation	RELU

Table 3.15: Hyper-parameters of the CNN and mDNN used on the ELISE dataset. The parameter values are given assuming that the input of the models is of size $T \times S$ where T is the length of the multichannel segments along the time axis and S the number of sensor channels. The time length of the segmented ELISE multichannel data frames is $T = 416$.

- Performing CNN-transfer yields notable improvements compared to not using any transfer, as shown by the boost in performances obtained in both subject-dependent and subject-independent configurations by mCNN CNN-transfer over mCNN TTO.

While this additional set of experiments highlighted the viability of the proposed CNN-transfer approach on one additional target dataset, it also showed the persistent difficulty to obtain proper classification performances with a DNN architecture on this dataset despite the application of transfer learning. While mCNN CNN-transfer yielded the best results in the subject-independent configuration, the overall classification performances remain mediocre for a four-class problem.

3.6.2 *PainMonit* - transfer for sensor-based pain recognition

CNN-transfer was also applied on the PainMonit dataset introduced in [72] and Section 1.2.3 for the classification of pain against no pain using GSR, EMG, respiration, BVP and ECG. Two configurations were tested in a subject-independent setup with a leave-one-subject-out cross validation: one using the temperature of the pain stimuli as labels, the others using the subjective pain ratings provided by the subjects using the CoVAS slider. The classification results of CNN-transfer were compared to three baselines: one based on HCF and one based on residual CNNs both reported in [72], and mCNN TTO. The hyper-parameters of all DNN-models were manually fine-tuned and are reported in Table 3.17. The same approach as the one reported in Section 3.4 was followed for multichannel architectures: the mDNN hyper-parameters were firstly optimised for TTO, and then re-used to perform CNN-transfer. All classification performances are reported in Table 3.16.

Label type	Temperature		*CoVAS*	
	Acc (%)	AF1 (%)	Acc (%)	Af1 (%)
HCF [72]	66.91	52.73	75.57	56.01
Residual CNN [72]	58.54	**56.27**	66.49	**59.10**
mCNN TTO	67.71	45.73	74.25	47.68
mCNN CNN-transfer	**69.28**	52.39	**77.92**	52.66

Table 3.16: Classification performances of "no pain" vs "pain" using the temperature and *CoVAS* labels of the *PainMonit* dataset. The reported evaluation metrics are averaged over all folds of the leave-one-subject-out cross validation. The best performance between HCF and DNN is highlighted in bold for both types of labels.

Model	Parameter	Value
sDNN (for both TTO and CNN-transfer)	· # conv. + pool. + act. blocks	3
	· Conv. kernel size	(11,1), (11,1), (12,1)
	· Conv. sliding stride	(1,1), (1,1), (1,1)
	· # conv. kernels	10, 10, 10
	· Max pool. size	(2,1), (2,1), (2,1)
	· Activation	RELU
mDNN (for both TTO and CNN-transfer)	· # dense layers	2
	· # neurons per layer	1000, 100
	· Activation	RELU

Table 3.17: Hyper-parameters of the mDNN used on the PainMonit dataset. The parameter values are given assuming that the input of the models is of size $T \times S$ where T is the length of the multichannel segments along the time axis and S the number of sensor channels. The time length of the segmented PainMonit multichannel data frames is $T = 250$.

The performances reported in Table 3.16 lead to the following main observations:

- The overall performances of all tested feature extraction approaches remain

124

poor in both labelling configurations which indicate the overall difficulty of the classification problem at hand on this dataset.

- The multichannel architectures do not yield significantly better performances than the residual CNN model proposed in [72]. While multichannel architectures obtain better average accuracies over the folds of the leave-one-subject-out cross validation, their AF1s are also lower than the one of residual CNN.

- Once again, CNN-transfer yields strictly better performances than not using any transfer, as evidenced by the superior accuracies and AF1 scores of mCNN CNN-transfer compared to mCNN TTO in all tested configurations.

It is hypothesised that the overall classification performances on this dataset remain mediocre for the reasons highlighted in Section 1.2.3: the binary classification of no pain against pain was shown to be a difficult problem in the literature due to the large overlap between no pain and low/medium pain. The benefits of the transfer learning approach proposed in the frame of this thesis can nevertheless still be observed on this dataset. Further experiments on a larger dataset with pain categories annotations (e.g. low, medium, high pain) would need to be carried out to improve classification performances.

Chapter 4

Conclusion

4.1 Summary

The increasing availability and affordability of wearable sensors has simplified the process of acquiring data in a non-intrusive way, and opened new possibilities in various fields of ubiquitous computing. This thesis is devoted to the exploration of more powerful machine learning algorithms able to take advantage of the increasing amount of available time-series data. More specifically, it proposed to explore the topic of time-series classification using DNNs for various applications of ubiquitous computing. The thesis has in particular attempted to provide some elements of answer to the two following specific questions highlighted in Section 1.3:

Superiority of deep learning to traditional machine learning: Considering the difficulty to train such models in practice, is the application of deep learning beneficial for ubiquitous computing applications compared to more traditional machine learning approaches?

Enhancing deep feature learning on time-series data with transfer learning: Is it possible to propose a general deep transfer learning method that would enhance the performances of DNNs for ubiquitous computing applications where data are limited?

The studies to answer those two questions described in the previous Sections can be summarised as follows:

Superiority of deep learning to traditional machine learning: The question of whether deep learning can provide benefits over traditional approaches relying on feature engineering was investigated for three different applications of ubiquitous computing: sensor-based HAR, emotion recognition and pain recognition. The results of the studies carried out highlighted that deep feature learning is not always the best approach, as traditional feature engineering remains state-of-the-art on some of the tested datasets, in particular for sensor-based pain recognition. In the frame of this thesis, the potential of deep feature learning for time-series classification was further explored for sensor-based HAR. The latter is one of the most popular application fields of

127

ubiquitous computing due to the widespread availability of movement-based sensors (e.g. IMUs) which have simplified the data collection process. This led to a higher quantity of available data compared to other application fields of ubiquitous computing, and consequently fostered the search for efficient machine learning - and more specifically feature learning - algorithms. In the frame of this thesis, a comparative study of feature learning methods was carried out on two benchmark datasets of sensor-based HAR: the OPPORTUNITY and UniMiB-SHAR datasets. Various DNN architectures were tested on both datasets and compared to state-of-the-art approaches using HCF found in the past HAR literature. The results of the study highlighted two main phenomena: the superiority of features learned by DNNs over HCF, and the reliability of hybrid DNN architectures involving convolutional and LSTM layers for HAR. Such results indicate the potential of deep learning for time-series classification when enough data of sufficient quality are available.

Enhancing deep feature learning on time-series data with transfer learning: To help address data scarcity issues which are common when dealing with ubiquitous computing applications, a new transfer learning method for DNNs trained for time-series classification was proposed. Inspired by successful deep transfer learning techniques involving images, the method presented in this thesis proposes to use recognition of sensor modalities in time-series data as an auxiliary task to learn useful general time-series features. A source dataset aggregating various time-series datasets related to diverse ubiquitous computing applications is firstly built: the multichannel data records are split into single-channel segments and labelled with their sensor modality information. A single-channel DNN (sDNN) is then trained for sensor modality recognition and the source dataset. In a second phase, the weights of the sDNN are then transferred to a multichannel DNN architecture (mDNN) processing data of the target dataset. The mDNN is finally fine-tuned on the target domain to solve the target task. Compared to previous time-series transfer learning approaches proposed in the literature, the method of this thesis can be applied to multichannel data which are encountered in most real-life applications, and could potentially be applied to any ubiquitous computing application using time-series data. Experiments were carried out using four datasets containing a high diversity of sensor modalities to build the source domain (OPPORTUNITY, gas-mixture, energy-appliance, EEG-eye-state), and two target datasets acquired for distinct applications: CogAge for sensor-based HAR and DEAP for sensor-based ER. Their results showed that the proposed transfer approach could yield better classification performances than not using any transfer on both target datasets indicating its promising potential for time-series classification using DNNs.

To summarise the aforementioned comments: the findings of this thesis highlight that deep learning should not necessarily be considered as a default option for time-series classification. They, however, also show the strong potential of DNNs as feature learners for time-series data, as seen by their superiority over traditional methods for sensor-based HAR. Finally, the studies involving the new deep transfer learning time-series approach proposed in the frame of this thesis hint at its superiority compared to not using any transfer, and suggest that using sensor modality classification is effective as an auxiliary task to learn general transferable features.

4.2 Limitations

This thesis provided elements of answer to the questions raised in Section 1.3 regarding whether applying DNNs for time-series classification was relevant when data are scarce, and whether it could be possible to enhance DNN performances using time-series transfer learning. Despite providing promising results, the studies presented in Sections 2 and 3 have several limitations which require further exploration. The most important ones are summarised as follows:

- **Limited scope of the comparative feature learning studies:** the superiority of DNNs over other feature extraction approaches was only strictly demonstrated in the context of sensor-based HAR. The data collection process is significantly easier for sensor-based HAR than other applications of ubiquitous computing due to how cheap and widespread motions sensors such as IMUs are, and due to the fact that obtaining objective data annotations characterising the subjects' gestures is relatively simple. Those factors have led to a relatively high availability of labelled data, which established favourable conditions for the development of machine learning approaches - including deep learning. Additional experiments were also carried out in this thesis on other application fields of ubiquitous computing where obtaining data is much more complex, such as sensor-based ER or PR. The results presented in Sections 1.2.2, 1.2.3, 3.6.1 and 3.6.2 showed that while DNNs could obtain comparable performances to other feature extraction approaches, they could, however, not lead to a significant improvement in performances compared to them. In order to establish a clear superiority of DNNs for those specific applications, studies with much larger amounts of data would be required, but this task is complicated by the lack of currently existing large-scale datasets.

- **Limited scope of the proposed transfer learning approach:** due to time limitations, the experiments carried out in Section 3 had to be constrained to a limited number of applications and associated datasets: four time-series datasets covering various applications (OPPORTUNITY, Gas-mixture, Energy-appliance prediction and EEG-eye-state) were used to constitute a source dataset for the proposed transfer learning approach. The effectiveness of the latter was then checked on four different target datasets: CogAge (HAR), DEAP (ER), ELISE (ER), PainMonit (PR). Checking if the proposed method would still work after adding more datasets to the source domain or after using a different target domain would be needed to further validate its generalisation capacity. Additionally, the experiments carried out in this thesis included only "regular" time-series data. It could be interesting to check if the proposed transfer approach still works with different types of data such as binary event-based or asynchronous time-series in either the source dataset, the target dataset or both. Finally, it is worth noting that only convolutional-based DNN models have been tested in the transfer learning experiments, following findings in the literature highlighting their ability to learn strong features in time-series data no matter the application domain [154]. Other types of DNNs (e.g. MLP, LSTM, hybrid) could be tested in the future to check if they are also compatible with the proposed transfer method.

- **Difficulties to understand why the proposed transfer strategy works:** the experiments carried out in Section 3.4.4 showed that transferring the features learned by the sDNN allowed the mDNN to learn more relevant features in data which mattered the most for the classification problem (e.g. smartwatch and smartphone data). This suggests that the time-series features learned on the source dataset were general enough to be successfully re-adapted to the target domain. Those experiments however neither strictly prove such hypothesis, nor provide explanation of why sensor modality classification could work as source task. It can be noted that this last question was further explored in additional (unpublished) preliminary experiments based on the ideas of Fawaz et al. [158] - mentioned in Section 3.2.2 - who hypothesised that successful time-series transfer learning could happen when the source and target datasets are "close enough". The proposed approach of [158] was re-adapted in the transfer learning experimental setup described in Section 3 to compute the DTW distances each source and target datasets. The results of those experiments highlighted some counter-intuitive phenomena, such as the fact that the closest source dataset to the target one was not necessarily the one containing the most similar sensor modalities. For instance, the energy-appliance dataset is closer to CogAge than the HAR dataset OPPORTUNITY, or the EEG-eye-state dataset is the furthest of the four source datasets to DEAP (which mostly contains EEG data) as shown in Table 4.1. In addition, good transfer performances could still be obtained using only source datasets still far from the target ones, as indicated by the relatively good performances of CNN-transfer using only the gas-mixture and EEG-eye-state datasets to build the source domain in Tables 4.2 and 4.3. The difficulty to provide an explanation to why CNN-transfer works using state-of-the-art techniques illustrates how understanding the exact mechanisms behind why transfer learning works still remains an open research question as of today.

d(source, target)	Target dataset		
Source dataset	CogAge BBH	DEAP arousal	DEAP Valence
OPPORTUNITY (OPP)	2,969.19	3,161.53	3,576.81
Gas-mixture (GM)	3,658.18	3,532.40	3,517.92
EEG-eye-state (EES)	518,731.06	536,890.62	527,820.44
Energy-appliance (EA)	1,091.90	1,467.24	1,290.96

Table 4.1: DTW distances between source and target datasets using the approach of Fawaz et al. [158]. Average time-series sequences s_i were computed on all time-series of each sensor modality present in a source dataset $\mathcal{S}$ using DBA. Average time-series sequences t_j were computed for each class and sensor modality present in a target dataset $\mathcal{T}$. The distance between $\mathcal{S}$ and $\mathcal{T}$ is defined as $d(\mathcal{S}, \mathcal{T}) = \min_{i,j} DTW(s_i, t_j)$.

Source dataset(s)	Acc (%)	AF1 (%)	MAP (%)
OPP+GM+EES+EA	71.95	71.72	75.03
OPP+GM+EES	62.01	61.80	66.31
GM+EES	66.99	66.52	72.37
EES[1]	63.72	63.64	66.29

Table 4.2: Performances of CNN-transfer for CogAge BBH using different source datasets. Source datasets were removed in increasing order of distance with the target dataset.

Source dataset(s)	Acc Arousal (%)	Acc Valence (%)
OPP+GM+EES+EA	91.29	90.64
OPP+GM+EES	82.13	78.24
OPP+EES	82.17	79.82
GM+EES	89.91	90.33
EES[1]	80.67	80.87

Table 4.3: Performances of CNN-transfer on DEAP using different source datasets. Source datasets were removed in increasing order of distance with the target dataset. Note: the distance between the DEAP, Gas-mixture and OPPORTUNITY datasets varies depending on the type of labels used on DEAP.

---

[1]The EEG-eye-state contains a single sensor modality (EEG). In this configuration, CNN-transfer was applied by training the sDNN as binary classifier to recognise between EEG and "other" sensor modalities. Data from the other three source datasets (OPPORTUNITY, Gas-mixture, Energy-appliance was used to form the class "other".

4.3 Future work

The following directions could be investigated in order to expand the scope of the thesis contents and attempt to address some of the thesis limitations previously raised:

- **Extension of the comparative study to other ubiquitous computing applications:** the application field of sensor-based HAR was chosen to carry out the comparative studies between DNNs and other feature extraction approaches in this thesis due to its relative importance for ubiquitous computing, and its relatively higher availability of data. Additional comparative experiments in other application fields could be carried out to verify the superiority of deep learning feature learning over traditional feature engineering. Similar attempts have for instance recently been made for sensor-based PR on the *BioVid* benchmark dataset [90] where Thiam et al. [185] showed that CNN-based feature learners could outperform carefully designed HCF for the classification of no pain against various pain levels. But the scope of this study is limited by the fact that only one pain dataset was tested, and that no concrete proof of the benefits of DNNs over traditional feature engineering on other pain datasets has emerged in the literature so far. The same problem has been observed for other ubiquitous computing applications such as sensor-based ER. For those applications, testing on additional datasets would be required.

- **Testing additional transfer learning configurations for the proposed approach:** because of time constraints, the proposed transfer learning approach could be tested on a limited number of datasets only and with a limited amount of transfer configurations. Additional experiments could be carried out to check how robust CNN-transfer is. Testing the approach on other target domains - in particular not related to sensor-based HAR, ER or PR - would be useful to check whether it can consistently generalise to any ubiquitous computing application requiring time-series data. Using additional datasets to build the source domain could also be performed to check how increasing the number of modalities or how the granularity of the source classes affect the transfer performances, akin to what was already done for transfer learning on ImageNet [46]. Adding different types of time-series data in either the source, target domain or both such as asynchronous time-series (e.g. GPS data), event-based time-series (e.g. eye blinking data from smartglasses), etc., could also be done to check whether CNN-transfer can also work for ubiquitous computing approaches using such data. Finally, the proposed transfer learning approach could also be tested with different types of DNNs. CNNs were used in the experiments of this thesis since they proved to be reliable feature learners on time-series for a large variety of target application fields [155, 158, 154]. The encouraging performances of other deep learning models for some specific applications - such as LSTM for HAR [8, 155, 10] - could be an incentive to test the proposed transfer approach with such models.

Bibliography

[1] M. Weiser. The computer for the 21st century, 1988. `https://web.archive.org/web/20141022035044/http://www.ubiq.com/hypertext/weiser/SciAmDraft3.html`.

[2] A. Krizhevstky, I. Sutskever, and G. E. Hinton. ImageNet classification with deep convolutional neural networks. In *NIPS*, 2012.

[3] J. Deng, W. Dong, R. Socher, L. Li, K. Li, and L. Fei-Fei. ImageNet: a large-scale hierarchical image database. In *CVPR*, 2009.

[4] R. Girshick, J. Donahue, T. Darell, and J. Malik. Rich feature hierachies for accurate object detection and segmentation. In *CVPR*, 2014.

[5] J. Donahue, Y. Jia, O. Vinyals, J. Hoffman, N. Zhang, E. Tzeng, and T. Darell. DeCAF: a deep convolutional activation feature for generic visual recognition. In *ICML*, 2014.

[6] M. Oquab, L. Bottou, I. Laptev, and J. Sivic. Learning and transferring mid-level image representation using convolutional neural networks. In *CVPR*, 2014.

[7] P. Sermanet, D. Eigen, X. Zhang, M. Mathieu, R. Fergus, and Y. LeCun. OverFeat: Integrated recognition, localization and detection using convolutional networks. In *Proc. of ICLR*, 2014.

[8] N. Y. Hammerla, S. Halloran, T. Plötz, and T. Deep. Deep convolutional and recurrent models for human activity recognition using wearables. In *IJCAI*, 2016.

[9] F. J. Ordonez and D. Roggen. Deep convolutional and lstm recurrent neural networks for multimodal wearable activity recognition. *Sensors*, 16(115), 2016.

[10] F. Li, K. Shirahama, M. A. Nisar, L. Köping, and M. Grzegorzek. Comparison of feature learning methods for human activity recognition using wearable sensors. *Sensors*, 18(2), 2018.

[11] G. Moore. Cramming more components onto integrated circuits. *Electronics*, 38(8), 1965.

[12] M. Weiser. Computer science challenges for the next 10 years, 1996. `https://www.youtube.com/watch?v=7jwLWosmmjE`.

[13] G. Manogaran and D. Lopez. A survey of big data architecture and machine learning algorithms in healthcare. *Biomedical Engineering and Technology*, 25:182–211, 2017.

[14] S. D'Mello and A. Graesser. Autotutor and affective autotutor: Learning by talking with cognitively and emotionally intelligent computers that talk back. *ACM Transactions of Interactive Intelligent Systems*, pages 2287–2293, 2013.

[15] B. Pogorelc, Z. Bosnić, and M. Gams. Automatic recognition of gait-related health problems in the elderly using machine learning. *Multimedia Tools and Applications*, 58:333–354, 2012.

[16] L. Breiman. Bias, variance and arcing classifiers, 1996. technical report.

[17] A. L. Samuel. Some studies in machine learning using the game of checkers. *IBM Journal of Research and Development*, 3(3), 1959.

[18] R. Dechter. Learning while searching in constraint-satisfaction-problems. In *AAAI*, 1986.

[19] R. Memisevic, C. Zach, M. Pollefeys, and G. E. Hinton. Gated softmax classification. In *NIPS*, 2010.

[20] X. Glorot and Y. Bengio. Understanding the difficulty of training deep feed-forward neural networks. In *Proc. of AISTATS*, pages 249–256, 2010.

[21] D. E. Rumelhart, G. E. Hinton, and R. J. Williams. Learning internal representations by back-propagating errors. *Nature*, 323(6088):533–536, 1986.

[22] W. S. McCullogh and W. Pitts. A logical calculus of the ideas immanent in nervous activity. *The Bulletin of Mathematical Biophysics*, 5:115–133, 1943.

[23] F. F. Rosenblatt. The perceptron: a probabilistic model for information storage and organisation in the brain. *Psychological Review*, 1958.

[24] A. Ivakhnenko and V. Lapa. *Cybernetics and Forecasting Techniques*. American Elsevier, 1967.

[25] P. Werbos. Beyond regression: New tools for prediction and analysis in the behavioural sciences. PhD thesis, 1974.

[26] D. C. Ciresan, U. Meier, L. M. Gambardella, and J. Schmidhuber. Deep, big, simple neural nets for handwritten digits recognition. *Neural Computation*, 22(12):3207–3220, 2010.

[27] G. Cybenko. Approximation by superposition of a sigmoidal function. *Mathematics of Signals, Controls and Systems*, 2:303–314, 1989.

[28] I. Goodfellow, Y. Bengio, and A. Courville. *Deep Learning*. MIT Press, 2016. http://www.deeplearningbook.org.

[29] K. Fukushima. Neocognitron: a self-organising neural network model for a mechanism of pattern recognition unaffected by shift in position. *Biological Cybernetics*, 36(4):193–202, 1980.

[30] Y. LeCun, B. Boser, J. S. Denker, D. Henderson, R. E. Howard, W. Hubbard, and L. D. Jackel. Backpropagation applied to handwritten zip code recognition. *Neural Computation*, 1:541–551, 1989.

[31] S. Hochreiter and J. Schidhuber. Long short-term memory. *Neural Computation*, 9(8):1735–1780, 1997.

[32] M. D. Zeiler and R. Fergus. Visualising and understanding convolutional networks. In *ECCV*, 2013.

[33] Y. Bengio, A. Courville, and P. Vincent. Representation learning: a review and new perspectives. *IEEE Transactions on Pattern Analysis and Machine Intelligence*, 35(8):1798–1828, 2013.

[34] C. Cortes and V. Vapnik. Support vector networks. *Machine Learning*, 20:273–297, 1995.

[35] L. Breiman, J. Friedman, C. J. Stone, and R. A. Olshen. *Classification and Regression Trees*. Taylor & Francis, 1984.

[36] K. Simonyan and A. Zisserman. Very deep convolutional networks for large-scale image recognition. In *Proc. of ICLR*, 2015.

[37] Y. Bengio. Gradient-based optimisation of hyperparameters. *Neural Computation*, 12(8):1889–1900, 2000.

[38] T. Domham, J. T. Springenberg, and F. Hutter. Speeding up automatic hyperparameter optimisation of deep neural networks by extrapolation of learning curves. In *AAAI*, 2015.

[39] D. MacLaurin, D. Duvenaud, and R. P. Adams. Gradient-based hyperparameter optimisation through reversible learning. In *ICML*, 2015.

[40] K. Simonyan, A. Vevaldi, and A. Zisserman. Deep inside convolutional networks: Visualising image classification models and saliency maps. arXiv:1312.6034, 2013.

[41] R. R. Selvaraju, M. Cogswell, A. Das, R. Vedantam, D. Parikh, and D. Batra. Grad-CAM: Visual explanations from deep networks via gradient-based localisation. In *ICCV*, 2017.

[42] Y. N. Dauphin and Y. Bengio. Big neural networks waste capacity. arXiv:1301.3583, 2013.

[43] C. Lin, Z. Song, H. Song, Y. Zhou, Y. Wang, and G. Wu. Differential privacy preserving in big data analytics for connected health. *Journal of Medical Systems*, 40(97), 2016.

[44] S. J. Pan and Q. Yang. A survey on transfer learning. *IEEE Transactions on Knowledge and Data Engineering*, 22(10):1345–1359, 2009.

[45] J. Yosinski, J. Clune, Y. Bengio, and H. Lipson. How transferable are features in deep neural networks? In *Proc. of NIPS*, volume 27, pages 3320–3328, 2014.

[46] M. Huh, P. Agrawal, and A. A. Efros. What makes ImageNet good for transfer learning? In *CVPR*, 2016.

[47] S. Dubois, N. Romano, K. Jung, N. Shah, and D. C. Kale. The effectiveness of transfer learning in electronic health records data. In *Proc. of ICLR Workshop*, 2017.

[48] F. J. O. Morales and D. Roggen. Deep convolutional feature transfer across mobile activity recognition domains, sensor modalities and locations. In *Proc. of ISWC*, pages 92–99, 2016.

[49] A. H. Khan, N. Roy, and A. Misra. Scaling human activity recognition via deep learning-based domain adaptation. In *Proc. of PERCOM*, 2018.

[50] J. Wang, Y. Chen, L. Hu, X. Peng, and P. S. Yu. Stratified transfer learning for cross-domain activity recognition. In *Proc. of PERCOM*, 2018.

[51] P. Malhotra, V. TV, L. Vig, P. Agarwal, and G. Shroff. TimeNet: Pre-trained deep recurrent neural networks for time series classification. In *Proc. of ESANN*, 2017.

[52] D. Krönert, A. Grünewald, F. Li, M. Grzergozek, and R. Brück. Sensor headband for emotion recognition in a virtual reality environment. In *ITIB*, 2018.

[53] A. Grünewald, F. Li, H. Kampling, D. Krönert, J. Pöhler, J. Littau, K; Schnieber, A. Piet, R. Brück, B. Niehaves, and M. Grzergozek. Biomedical data acquisition and processing to recognize emotions for affective learning. In *IEEE BIBE*, 2018.

[54] N. Takashima, F. Li, M. Grzegorzek, and K. Shirahama. Cross-modal music-emotion retrieval using DeepCCA. In *ITIB*, 2020.

[55] R. W. Picard. *Affective Computing*. The MIT Press, 2000.

[56] P. Ekman. An argument for basic emotions. *Cognition & Emotions*, 6(3):169–200, 1992.

[57] R. Plutchik. The nature of emotions. *American Scientist*, 89(4):344–350, 2001.

[58] J. A. Russell. A circumplex model of affect. *Journal of Personality and Social Psychology*, 39(6):1161–1178, 1980.

[59] W. Wen, G. Liu, N. Cheng, J. Wei, P. Shangguan, and W. Huang. Emotion recognition based on multi-variant correlation of physiological signals. *IEEE Transactions on Affective Computing*, 5(2):126–140, 2014.

[60] M. Liu, D. Fan, X. Zhang, and X. Gong. Human emotion recognition based on galvanic skin response, signal feature selection and SVM. In *IEEE ICSCSE*, 2016.

[61] W. Zheng. Multichannel EEG-based emotion recognition via group sparse canonical correlation analysis. *IEEE Transactions on Cognitive and Developmental Systems*, 9(3):281–290, 2017.

[62] J. D. Mayer, J. P. Allen, and K. Beauregard. Mood inductions for four specific moods: a procedure employing guided imagery vignettes with music. *Journal of Mental Imagery*, 19(1):151–159, 1995.

[63] A. Markey, A. Chin, and E. M. Vanepps. Identifying a reliable boredom induction. *Perceptual and Motor Skills*, 119(1), 2014.

[64] E. A. Berg. A simple objective technique for measuring flexibility in thinking. *Journal of General Psychology*, 39:15–22, 1948.

[65] R. Palermo, K. B. O'Connor, J. M. Davis, J. Irons, and E. McKone. New tests to measure individual differences in matching and labelling facial expressions of emotions, and their associations with ability to recognise vocal emotions and facial identity. *PLoS One*, 8(6), 2013.

[66] S. Koelstra, C. Mühl, M. Soleymani, J. Lee, A. Yazdani, T. Ebrahimi, T. Pun, A. Nijholt, and I. Patras. DEAP: a database for emotion analysis using physiological signals. *IEEE Transactions on Affective Computing*, 3:18–31, 2011.

[67] S. Tripathi, S. Acharya, R. D. Sharma, S. Mittal, and S. Bhattacharya. Using deep and convolutional neural networks for accurate emotion classification on DEAP dataset. In *IAAI*, 2017.

[68] X. Li, P. Zhang, D. Song, G. Yu, Y. Hou, and B. Hu. EEG based emotion identification using unsupervised deep feature learning. In *SIGIR*, 2015.

[69] W. Liu, W. Zheng, and B. Lu. Emotion recognition using multimodal deep learning. In *ICONIP*, 2016.

[70] J. Scheirer, R. Fernandez, J. Klein, and R. W. Picard. Frustrating the user on purpose: a step towards building an affective computer. *Interacting with Computers*, 14:93–118, 2002.

[71] M. D. Zeiler. ADADELTA: an adaptive learning rate method, 2012.

[72] P. J. Gouverneur, F. Li, T. M. Szikszay, W. M. Adamczyk, K. Lüdtke, and M. Grzegorzek. Classification of heat-induced pain using physiological signals. In *ITIB*, 2020.

[73] H. Merskey. Pain terms: a list with denitions and notes on usage. recommended by theIASP subcommittee on taxonomy. *Pain*, 6(249), 1979.

[74] R. Melzack. The short-form McGill pain questionnaire. *Pain*, 30(2):191–197, 1987.

[75] C. S. Cleeland and K. M. Ryan. Pain assessment: Global use of the brief pain inventory. *Annals of Academy of Medicine*, 23(2):129–138, 1994.

[76] B. Ambuel, K. W. hamlett, C. M. Marx, and J. L. Blumer. Assessing distress in pediatric intensive care environments: the COMFORT scale. *Journal of Pediatric Psychology*, 17(1):95–109, 1992.

[77] A. Salah and M. I. Khalil. Multimodal pain level recognition using majority voting technique. In *ICCES*, 2018.

[78] P. Thiam, V. Kessler, M. Amirian, P. Bellmann, G. Layher, Y. Zhang, M. Velana, S. Gruss, S. Walter, H. C. Traue, J. Kim, D. Schork, E. André, H. Neumann, and F. Schwenker. Multi-modal pain intensity recognition based on the SenseEmotion database. *IEEE Transactions on Affective Computing*, 2019.

[79] P. Werner, A. Al-Hamadi, R. Niese, S. Walter, S. Gruss, and H. C. Traue. Automatic pain recognition from video and biomedical signals. In *ICPR*, 2014.

[80] D. Lopez-Martinez and R. Picard. Multi-task neural networks for personalised pain recognition from physiological signals. In *ACII Workshops and Demos*, 2017.

[81] D. Lopez-Martinez and R. Picard. Continuous pain intensity estimation from autonomic signals with recurrent neural networks. In *IEEE EMBC*, 2018.

[82] R. Zhi and J. Yu. Multi-modal fusion based automatic assessment. In *IEEE ITAIC*, 2019.

[83] Y. Wu and Q. Ji. Facial landmark detection: a literature survey. *International Journal on Computer Vision*, 2017.

[84] P. Werner, A. Al-Hamadi, K. Limbrecht-Ecklund, S. Walter, S. Gruss, and H. C. Traue. Automatic pain assessment with facial activity descriptors. *IEEE Transactions on Affective Computing*, 8(3):286–299, 2016.

[85] J. O. Ogede and M. Valstar. Cumulative attributes for pain intensity estimation. In *ICMI*, 2017.

[86] E. Othman, P. Werner, F. Saxen, A. Al-Hamadi, and S. Walter. Cross-database evaluation of pain recognition from facial video. In *ISPA*, 2019.

[87] A. Semwal and N. D. Londhe. Automated pain severity detection using convolutional neural networks. In *CTEMS*, 2018.

[88] R. Theagarajan, B. Bhanu, D. Angeles, and F. Pala. KnowPain: Automated system for detecting pain in neonates from videos. In *MCS*, 2018.

[89] M. Tavakolian and A. Hadid. A spatiotemporal convolutional neural network for automatic pain intensity estimation from facial dynamics. *International Journal of Computer Vision*, 127:1413–1425, 2019.

[90] S. Walter, S. Gruss, H. Ehleiter, J. Tan, H. C. Traue, P. Werner, A. Al-Hamadi, S. Crawcour, A. O. Andrade, and G. M. da Silva. The BioVid heat pain database: Data for the advancement and systematic validation of an automated pain recognition system. In *IEEE CYCONF*, 2013.

[91] M. A. Haque, R. B. Bautista, F. Noroozi, K. Kulkarni, C. B. Laursen, R. Irani, M. Bellantonio, S. Escalera, G. Anbarjafari, K. Nasrollahi, O. K. Andersen, E. G. Spaich, and T. B. Moeslund. Deep multimodal pain recognition: a database and comparison of spatio-temporal visual modalities. In *IEEE ICAFGR*, 2018.

[92] M. Kächele, P. Werner, A. Al-Hamadi, G. Palm, S. Walter, and F. Schwenker. Bio-visual fusion for person-independent recogntion of pain. In *MCS*, 2015.

[93] M. Kächele, P. Thiam, M. Amirian, F. Scwenker, and G. Palm. Methods for person-centered continuous pain intensity assessment from bio-physiological channels. *IEEE Journal of Selected Topics in Signal Processing*, 10(5):854–864, 2016.

[94] Y. Chu, X. Zhao, J. Han, and Y. Su. Physiological signal-based method for measurement of pain intensity. *Frontiers in Neuroscience*, 2017.

[95] P. Werner, A. Al-Hamadi, R. Niese, and S. Walter. Towards pain monitoring: Facial expression, head pose, a new database, an automatic system and remaining challenges. In *BMVC*, 2013.

[96] M. Velana, S. Gruss, G. Layher, P. Thiam, Y. Zhang, D. Schork, V. Kessler, S. Meudt, H. Neumann, J. Kim, F. Schwenker, and E. Andre. The SenseEmotion database: a multimodal database for the development and systematic validation of an automatic pain - and emotion recognition system. In *MPRSS*, 2017.

[97] P. Werner, A. Al-Hamadi, S. Gruss, and S. Walter. Twofold-multimodal pain recognition with the X-ITE pain database. In *ACIIW*, 2019.

[98] D. Lopez-Martinez, O. Rudovic, and R. Picard. Physiological and behavioural profiling for nociceptive pain estimation using personalised multitask learning. In *NIPS*, 2017.

[99] K. He, X. Zhang, S. Ren, and J. Sun. Deep residual learning for image recognition. In *CVPR*, 2016.

[100] M. Jiang, R. Mieronkoski, E. Syrjälä, A. Anzanpour, V. Terävä, A. M. Rahamani, S. Salaterä, R. Aantaa, N. Hagelberg, and P. Lijeberg. Acute pain intensity monitoring with the classification of multiple physiological parameters. *Journal of Clinical Monitoring and Computing*, 33(3), 2019.

[101] H. Lim, B. Kim, G. Noh, and S. R. Yoo. A deep neural network-based pain classifier using a photoplethysmography signal. *Sensors*, 19(2), 2019.

[102] F. Li, K. Shirahama, M. A. Nisar, X. Huang, and M. Grzegorzek. Deep transfer learning for time series data based on sensor modality classification. *Sensors*, 20(15), 2020.

[103] R. Chavarriaga, H. Sagha, A. Calatroni, S. Digumarti, G. Tröster, J. d. R. Millán, and D. Roggen. The opportunity challenge: A benchmark database for on-body sensor-based activity recognition. *Pattern Recognition Letters*, 34(15):2033–2042, 2013.

[104] D. Micucci, M. Mobilio, and P. Napoletano. UniMiB SHAR: a new dataset for human activity recognition using acceleration data from smartphones. *Applied Sciences*, 7(1101), 2016.

[105] S. W. G. Derbyshire, A. K. P. Jones, F. Gyulai, S. Clark, D. Townsend, and L. L. Firestone. Pain processing during three levels of noxious stimulation produces different patterns of central activity. *Pain*, 73(3):431–445, 1997.

[106] J. K. Aggarwal M. S. Ryoo. Recognition of composite human activities through context-free grammar-based representation. In *CVPR*, 2006.

[107] O. D. Lara and M. A. Labrador. A survey on human activity recognition using wearable sensors. *IEEE Communications Surveys and Tutorials*, 15:1192–1209, 2013.

[108] P. Zappi, T. Stiefmeier, E. Farella, D. Roggen, L. Benini, and G. Troster. Activity recognition from on-body sensors by classifier fusion: sensor scalability and robustness. In *IEEE International Conference on Intelligent Sensors, Sensor Networks and Information*, 2007.

[109] A. M. Nisar, K. Shirahama, F. Li, X. Huang, and M. Grzegorzek. Rank pooling approach for wearable sensor-based ADLs recognition. *Sensors*, 20(12), 2020.

[110] L. Chen, J. Hoey, C. D. Nugent, D. J. Cook, and Z. Yu. Sensor-based activity recognition. *IEEE Transactions on systems, man and cybernetics, part C*, 42:790–808, 2012.

[111] S. R. Ke, H. L. U. Thuc, Y. J. Lee, J. N. Hwang, J. H. Yoo, and K. H. Choi. A review on video-based human activity recognition. *Computers*, 2(2):88–131, 2013.

[112] D. J. Cook and N. C. Krishnan. *Activity learning; discovering, recognizing and predicting human behavior from sensor data*. Wiley, 2015.

[113] A. Bulling, U. Blanke, and B. Schiele. Tutorial on human activity recognition using body-worn inertial sensors. *ACM Computing Surveys*, 46:1–33, 2014.

[114] M. F. A. b. Abdullah, A. F. P. Negara, M. S. Sayeed, D. J. Choi, and K. S. Muthu. Classification algorithms in human activity recognition using smartphones. *International Journal of Biomedical and Biological Engineering*, 6(8):362–369, 2012.

[115] L. Breiman. Random forests. *Machine Learning*, 45:5–32, 2001.

[116] I. Rish. An empirical study of the naive bayes classifier. In *IJCAI Workshop on Empirical Methods in Artificial Intelligence*, 2001.

[117] R. Kohavi and D. H. Wolpert. Bias plus variance decomposition for zero-one loss functions. In *ICML*, 1996.

[118] R. W. Picard and J. Healey. Affective wearables. *Personal Technologies*, 1:231–240, 1997.

[119] U. Maurer, A. Smailagic, D. P. Siewiorek, and M. Deisher. Activity recognition and monitoring using multiple sensors on different body positions. In *International Workshop on Wearable and Implantable Body Sensor Networks*, 2006.

[120] L. Wang, T. Gu, X. Tao, and J. Lu. Sensor-based human activity recognition in a multi-user scenario. In *European Conference on Ambient Intelligence*, 2009.

[121] M. Zhang and A. A. Sawchuk. A feature selection-based framework for human activity recognition using wearable multimodal sensors. In *International Conference on Body Area Networks*, 2011.

[122] F. Attal, S. Mohammed, M. Dedabrishvili, F. Chamroukhi, L. Oukhellou, and Y. Amirat. Physical human activity recognition using wearable sensors. *Sensors*, 15(12), 2015.

[123] K. Kira and L. rendell. A practical approach to feature selection. In *ICML*, pages 249–256, 1992.

[124] N. A. Capela, E. D. Lemaire, and N. Baddour. Feature selection for wearable smartphone-based human activity recognition with able-bodied, elderly and stroke patients. *PLOS One*, 2015.

[125] D. Yandansepas, A. H. Niazi, J. L. Gay, F. W. Maier, L. Ramaswamy, K. Rasheed, and M. P. Buman. A multi-featured approach for wearable sensor-based human activity recognition. In *IEEE Conference on Healthcare Informatics*, 2016.

[126] A. Reiss and D. Stricker. Introducing a new benchmark dataset for activity monitoring. In *IEEE ISWC*, 2012.

[127] M. Bachlin, M. Plotnik, D. Roggen, I. Maiden, J. M. Hausdorff, N. Giladi, and G. Troster. Wearable assistant for parkinson's disease patients with the freezing of gait symptom. *IEEE Transactions on Information Technology in Biomedicine*, 14(2):436–446, 2010.

[128] D. Anguita, A. Ghio, L. Oneto, X. Parra, and J. L. Reyes-Ortiz. A public domain dataset for human activity recognition using smartphones. In *European Symposium on Artificial Neural Networks*, 2013.

[129] J. R. Kwapisz, G. M. Weiss, and S. A. Moore. Activity recognition using cell phone accelerometers. In *International Workshop on Knowledge Discovery from Sensor Data*, 2010.

[130] T. Plötz, N. Hammerla, and P. Olivier. Feature learning for activity recognition in ubiquitous computing. In *International Joint Conference on Artificial Intelligence*, 2011.

[131] R. Salakhutdinov, A. Mnih, and G. Hinton. Restricted boltzmann machines for collaborative filtering. In *ICML*, pages 791–798, 2007.

[132] J. Han, M. Kamber, and J. Pei. *Data Mining: concepts and Techniques*. Morgan Kaufmann, 2011.

[133] Y. Li, D. Shi, B. Ding, and D. Liu. Unsupervised feature learning for human activity recognition usign smartphone sensors. *Mining Intelligence and Knowledge Exploration*, 8891:99–107, 2014.

[134] D. E. Rumelhart, G. E. Hinton, and R. J. Williams. Learning internal representations by error propagation. *Parallel Distributed Processing*, 1, 1986.

[135] M. Zeng, L. T. Nguyen, B. Yu, O. J. Mengshoel, J. Zhu, P. Wu, and J. Zhang. Convolutional neural networks for human activity recognition using mobile sensors. In *IEEE International Conference on Mobile Computing, Applications and Services*, 2014.

[136] M. A. Alsheikh, A. Selim, D. Niyato, and L. Doyle. Deep activity recognition models with triaxial accelerometers. In *Workshop of the AAAI Conference on Artificial Intelligence*, 2015.

[137] G. E. Hinton, S. Osindero, and Y. W. Teh. A fast learning algorithm for deep belief networks. *Neural Computation*, 18(7):1527–1554, 2006.

[138] J. B. Yang, M. N. Nguyen, P. P. San, X. L. Li, and S. Krishnaswany. Deep convolutional neural network on multichannel time series for human activity recognition. In *IJCAI*, pages 3995–4001, 2015.

[139] Z. Chen, L. Zhang, Z. Cao, and J. Guo. Distilling the knowledge from handcrafted features for human activity recognition. *IEEE Transactions on Industrial Informatics*, 14(10):4334–4342, 2018.

[140] J. Wang, P. Liu, M. F. H. She, S. Nahavandi, and A. Kouzani. Bag-of-word representation for biomedical time-series classification. *Biomedical Signal Processing and Control*, 8(6):634–644, 2013.

[141] S. Bhattacharya, P. Nurni, N. Hammerla, and T. Plötz. Towards using un-labelled data in a sparse-coding framework for human-recognition. *Pervasive and Mobile Computing*, 15:242–262, 2014.

[142] K. Shirahama and M. Grzegorzek. On the generality of codebook approach for sensor-based human activity recognition. *Electronics*, 6(44), 2017.

[143] A. Krizhevstky, I. Sutskever, and G. E. Hinton. ImageNet classification with deep convolutional neural networks. In *NIPS*, pages 1097–1105, 2012.

[144] K. Chatfield, K. Simonyan, A. Vedaldi, and A. Zisserman. Return of the devil in the details: Delving deep into convolutional nets. In *BMVC*, 2014.

[145] A. L. Blum and P. Langley. Selection of relevant features and examples in machine learning. *Artificial Intelligence*, 97(1):245–271, 1997.

[146] G. Chandrashekar and F. Sahin. A survey on feature selection methods. *Computers and Electrical Engineering*, 40:16–28, 2014.

[147] J. Yang, Y.-G. Jiang, A. G. Hauptmann, and C. W. Ngo. Evaluating bag-of-visual-words representations in scene classification. In *MIR Workshop*, pages 197–206, 2007.

[148] M. G. Baydogan, G. Runger, and E. Tuv. A bag-of-features framework to classify time-series. *IEEE Transactions on Pattern Analysis and Machine Intelligence*, 35:2796–2802, 2013.

[149] J. Han, M. Kamber, and J. Pei. *Data Mining: Concepts and Techniques*. Morgan Kaufmann, 2011.

[150] J. C. van Gemert, C. J. Veenman, A. W. M. Smeulders, and J. M. Geusebroek. Visual word ambiguity. *IEEE Transactions on Pattern Analysis and Machine Intelligence*, 32:1271–1283, 2010.

[151] E. Nowak, F. Jurie, and B. Triggs. Sampling strategies for bag-of-features image classification. In *ECCV*, pages 490–503, 2016.

[152] S. Ioffe and C. Szegedy. Batch normalisation: Accelerating deep network training by reducing internal covariate shift. 2015. arXiv:1502.03167.

[153] Y. Saeys, T. Abeel, and Y. Van de Peer. Rebust feature selection using ensemble feature selection techniques. In *ECML*, number optional, pages 313–325, 2008.

[154] H. I. Fawaz, G. Forestier, J. Weber, L. Idoumghar, and P.-A. Muller. Deep learning for time series classification: a review. *Data Mining and Knowledge Discovery*, 33(4):917–963, 2019.

[155] J. Wang, Y. Chen, H. Hao, L. Hu, and X. Peng. Deep learning for sensor-based activity recognition: a survey. *Pattern Recognition Letters*, 119(1):3–11, 2018.

[156] X. Li, P. Zhang, D. Song, G. Yu, Y. Hou, and B. Hu. EEG-based emotion identification using unsupervised deep feature learning. In *Proc. of NeuroIR*, 2015.

[157] W. Liu, W.-L. Zheng, and B.-L. Lu. Multimodal emotion recognition using multimodal deep-learning. In *Proc. of ICONIP*, pages 521–529, 2016.

[158] H. I. Fawaz, G. Forestier, J. Weber, L. Idoumghar, and P.-A. Muller. Transfer learning for time-series classification. In *IEEE International Conference on Big Data*, 2018.

[159] L. Y. Pratt. Discriminatively-based transfer between neural networks. In *NIPS*, pages 204–211, 1993.

[160] M. J. Afridi, A. Ross, and E. M. Shapiro. On automated source selection for transfer learning in convolutional neural networks. *Pattern Recognition*, 73:65–75, 2018.

[161] R. Caruana. Multitask learning. *Machine Learning*, 28:41–75, 1997.

[162] C. Szegedy, W. Liu, Y. Jia, P. Sermanet, S. Reed, D. Anguelov, D. Erhan, V. Vanhoucke, and A. Rabinovich. Going deeper with convolutions. In *CVPR*, 2015.

[163] D. Yu, M. L. Seltzer, J. Li, J.-H. Huang, and F. Seide. Feature learning in deep neural networks - studies on speech recognition tasks. arXiv:1301.3605v3, 2013. Microsoft report.

[164] K. He, X. Zhang, S. Ren, and J. Sen. Deep residual learning for image recognition. In *Proc. of CVPR*, 2016.

[165] R. Girshick, J. Donahue, T. Darrell, and J. Malik. Rich feature hierarchies for accurate object detection and semantic segmentation. In *Proc. of CVPR*, pages 580–587, 2014.

[166] X. Yan, D. Acuna, and S. Fidler. Neural data server: a large-scale search engine for transfer learning data. In *CVPR*, 2020.

[167] Y. Guo, H. Shi, A. Kumar, K. Grauman, T. Rosing, and R. Feris. SpotTune: Transfer learning through adaptive fine-tuning. In *Proc. of CVPR*, 2019.

[168] X. Li, Y. Grandvalet, and F. Davoine. A baseline regularisation scheme for transfer learning with convolutional neural networks. *Pattern Recognition*, 98:.., 2019.

[169] D. Pathak, P. Krahenbuhl, J. Donahue, and A. A. Efros. Context encoders: Feature learning by inpainting. In *Proc. of CVPR*, 2016.

[170] Y. Chen, E. Keogh, B. Hu, N. Begum, A. Bagnall, A. Mueen, and G. Batista. The UCR time series classification archive. `www.cs.ucr.edu/~eamonn/time_series_data/`, 2015. Last accessed on 17/09/2019.

[171] D. Cook, K. D. Feuz, and N. C. Krishnan. Transfer learning for activity recognition: a survey. *Knowledge and Information Systems*, 36(3):537–556, 2013.

[172] D. Smirnov and E. M. Nguifo. Time-series classification with recurrent neural networks. In *Advanced Analytics and Learning on Temporal Data*, 2018.

[173] D. Dheeru and E. Karra Taniskidou. UCI machine learning repository. `http://archive.ics.uci.edu/ml`, 2017. Last accessed on 17/09/2019.

[174] J. Fonollosa, S. Sheik, R. Huerta, and S. Marco. Reservoir computing compensates slow response of chemosensor arrays exposed to fast varying gas concentrations in continuous monitoring. *Sensors and Actuators B: Chemical*, 215:618–629, 2015.

[175] O. Roesler. The EEG eye state dataset. `https://archive.ics.uci.edu/ml/datasets/EEG+Eye+State#`, 2013. Last accessed on 17/09/2019.

[176] L. M. Candanedo, V. Feldheim, and D. Deramaix. Data driven prediction models of energy use of appliances in a low-energy house. *Energy and Buildings*, 140(1):81–97, 2017.

[177] D. P. Kingma and M. Welling. Auto-encoding variational bayes. In *Proc. of ICML*, 2014.

[178] F. Chollet et al. Keras. `https://github.com/fchollet/keras`, 2015. Last accessed on 17/09/2019.

[179] I. Goodfellow et al. TensorFlow: Large-scale machine learning on heterogeneous systems. `http://tensorflow.org/`, 2015. Software available from tensorflow.org, last accessed on 17/09/2019.

[180] S. Jirayucharoensak, S. Pan-Ngum, and P. Israsena. EEG-based emotion recognition using deep learning network with principal component based covariate shift adaptation. *The Scientific World Journal*, 2014.

[181] X. Li, D. Song, P. Zheng, Y. Zheng, Y. Hou, and B. Hu. Exploring EEG features in cross-subject emotion recognition. *Frontiers in Neuroscience*, 12, 2019.

[182] R. Yu, A. Li, C. Chen, J. Lai V. I. Morariu, X. Han, M. Gao, and C. Lin. NISP: Pruning networks using neuron importance score propagation. In *Proc. of CVPR*, pages 9194–9203, 2018.

[183] G. Roffo, S. Melzi, and M. Cristani. Infinite feature selection. In *Proc. of ICCV*, pages 4202–4210, 2015.

[184] K. Simonyan, A. Vedaldi, and A. Zisserman. Deep inside convolutional networks: Visualising image classification models and saliency maps. In *ICLR Workshop*, 2014.

[185] P. Thiam, P. Bellmann, H. A. Kestler, and F. Schwenker. Exploring deep physiological models for nociceptive pain recognition. *Sensors*, 19(20), 2019.

List of own publications

The name(s) of the main author(s) for each publication is provided in bold.

[1] **Z. Boukhers**, K. Shirahama, <u>F. Li</u> and M. Grzegorzek, *Object Detection and Depth estimation for 3D Trajectory Extraction*, International Workshop on Content-Based Multimedia Indexing, 2015.

[2] **F. Li**, L. Köping, S. Schmitz and M. Grzegorzek, *Real-time Gesture Recognition Using a Particle Filtering Approach*, International Conference on Pattern Recognition Applications and Methods, 2017.

[3] **M. H. Khan**, <u>F. Li</u>, M. S. Farid and M. Grzegorzek, *Gait Recognition Using Motion Trajectory Analysis*, International Conference on Computer Recognition Systems, 2017.

[4] **D. Krönert**, A. Grünewald, <u>F. Li</u>, M. Grzegorzek and R. Brück, *Sensor Headband for Emotion Recognition in a Virtual Reality Environment*, International Conference on Information Technologies in Biomedicine, 2018.

[5] **A. Grünewald**, **D. Krönert**, J. Pöhler, **F. Li**, J. Littau, K. Schnieber, **H. Kampling**, B. Niehaves, M. Grzegorzek and R. Brück, *Biomedical data Acquisition and Processing to Recognize Emotions for Affective Learning*, IEEE Bioinformatics and Bioengineering, 2018.

[6] **N. Takashima**, <u>F. Li</u>, M. Grzegorzek and K. Shirahama, *Cross-modal Music-Emotion Retrieval Using DeepCCA*, International Conference on Information Technologies in Biomedicine, 2020.

[7] **P. Gouverneur**, <u>F. Li</u>, T. M. Szikszay, W. M. Adamczyk, K. Lüdtke and M. Grzegorzek, *Classification of Heat-Induced Pain Using Physiological Signals*, International Conference on Information Technologies in Biomedicine, 2020.

[8] **F. Li**, K. Shirahama, A. M. Nisar, L. Köping and M. Grzegorzek, *Comparison of Feature Learning Methods for Human Activity Recognition Using Wearable Sensors*, Sensors (MDPI), 18(679):1–22, 2018.

[9] **F. Li**, K. Shirahama, A. M. Nisar, X. Huang and M. Grzegorzek, *Deep Transfer Learning for Time Series Data Based on Sensor Modality Classification*, Sensors (MDPI), 20(15), 2020.

[10] **X. Huang**, K. Shirahama, <u>F. Li</u> and M. Grzegorzek, *Sleep Stage Classification for Child Patients using DeConvolutional Neural Network*, Artificial Intelligence in Medicine (Elsevier), 110, 2020.

List of abbreviations

Acc .... Accuracy
AE .... Autoencoder
AF1 .... Average F1-score
ANN .... Artificial Neural Network
ARC .... Activity Recognition Chain
BBH .... Behavioural Both Hands (activities)
BLHO .... Behavioural Left Hand Only (activities)
CBh .... Codebook approach with hard assignment
CBs .... Codebook approach with soft assignment
CogAge .... *Cognitive Village* (dataset)
CNN .... Convolutional Neural Network
DAE .... Denoising Autoencoder
DBA .... DTW Barycentre Averaging
DTW .... Dynamic Time Warping (distance)
DNN .... Deep Neural Network
ECG .... Electrocardiography
EEG .... Electroencephalography
EMG .... Electromyography
ER .... Emotion Recognition
GSR .... Galvanic Skin Response
HAR .... Human Activity Recognition
HCF .... Hand-Crafted Features
IMU .... Inertial Measurement Unit
LSTM .... Long-Short-Term Memory
mDNN .... Multichannel Deep Neural Network
MLP .... Multi-Layer Perceptron
PR .... Pain Recognition
PPG .... Photoplethysmography
RELU .... Rectified Linear Unit
sDNN .... Single Channel Deep Neural Network

List of Tables

List of Figures

Frédéric Li

French nationality
Born on 09/11/1991 in Nancy (France)

Education

2016 – now ▉ **Doctoral studies** - Institute of Medical Informatics, University of Lübeck, Germany (formerly: Research Group for Pattern Recognition, University of Siegen, Germany).
Thesis title: *Deep Learning for Time-series Classification Enhanced by Transfer Learning Based on Sensor Modality Discrimination*

2012 – 2015 ▉ **Engineer formation** - ENSTA ParisTech, Palaiseau, France.
Specialisation in Robotics and Embedded Systems.
Equivalent to Master of Science.

2009 – 2012 ▉ **Preparatory courses for engineering schools (CPGE)** - Janson de Sailly high school, Paris, France.
Specialisation in mathematics and physics.

2009 ▉ **Scientific Bachelor with honours** - Talma high school, Brunoy, France.

Work experiences

May 2016 – now ▉ **PhD candidate, lecturer & machine learning researcher** - Institute of Medical Informatics, Lübeck, Germany.
Studies on deep transfer learning based on sensor modality discrimination for time-series classification and processing using Deep Neural Networks.
Teaching in the Medical Data Science (bachelor) and Medical Data Science for Assistive Health Technologies (master).
Research and development for the *ELISE, Cognitive Village (CogAge)* and *PainMonit* projects (respective BMBF grant numbers: 16SV7512, 16SV7223K and 01DS19008B).

Oct. – Dec. 2015 ▉ **R&D engineer in machine learning** - Image Processing Department of Thales Optronics, Élancourt, France.
Research and development studies in machine learning for an automatic threat detection system in infrared images.

Apr. – Sept. 2015 ▉ **Trainee in machine learning** - Image Processing Department of Thales Optronics, Élancourt, France.
Statistic study of behavioural descriptors for a classification problem of potential threats in infrared images, using supervised learning methods.

May – Aug. 2014 ▉ **Research assistant** - Research Group for Pattern Recognition, Siegen, Germany.
Contribution to the development of an automatic event detection method in RGBD videos.

Aug. 2013 ▉ **English teacher in Kindergarten** - ChengYang My Best Kindergarten, Qingdao, China.